Mastering Python High Performance

Measure, optimize, and improve the performance of your Python code with this easy-to-follow guide

Fernando Doglio

PUBLISHING

BIRMINGHAM - MUMBAI

Mastering Python High Performance

First published: September 2015

Production reference: 1030915

Published by Packt Publishing Ltd.
Livery Place
35 Livery Street
Birmingham B3 2PB, UK.

ISBN 978-1-78398-930-0

www.packtpub.com

Credits

Author
Fernando Doglio

Reviewers
Erik Allik
Mike Driscoll
Enrique Escribano
Mosudi Isiaka

Commissioning Editor
Kunal Parikh

Acquisition Editors
Vivek Anantharaman
Richard Brookes-Bland

Content Development Editors
Akashdeep Kundu
Rashmi Suvarna

Technical Editor
Vijin Boricha

Copy Editors
Relin Hedly
Karuna Narayanan

Project Coordinator
Milton Dsouza

Proofreader
Safis Editing

Indexer
Mariammal Chettiyar

Graphics
Sheetal Aute

Production Coordinator
Arvindkumar Gupta

Cover Work
Arvindkumar Gupta

About the Author

Fernando Doglio has been working as a web developer for the past 10 years.

During that time, he shifted his focus to the Web and grabbed the opportunity of working with most of the leading technologies, such as PHP, Ruby on Rails, MySQL, Python, Node.js, AngularJS, AJAX, REST APIs, and so on.

In his spare time, Fernando likes to tinker and learn new things. This is why his GitHub account keeps getting new repos every month. He's also a big open source supporter and tries to win the support of new people with the help of his website, `lookingforpullrequests.com`.

You can reach him on Twitter at `@deleteman123`.

When he is not programming, he spends time with his family.

I'd like to thank my lovely wife for putting up with me and the long hours I spent writing this book; this book would not have been possible without her continued support. I would also like to thank my two sons. Without them, this book would've been finished months earlier.

Finally, I'd like to thank the reviewers and editors. They helped me get this book in shape and achieve the quality level that you deserve.

About the Reviewers

Erik Allik is a self-taught multilingual, multiparadigm full-stack software engineer. He started programming at the age of 14. Since then, Erik has been working with many programming languages (both imperative and functional) and various web and non-web-related technologies.

He has worked primarily with Python, Scala, and JavaScript. Erik is currently focusing on applying Haskell and other innovative functional programming techniques in various industries and leveraging the power of a mathematical approach and formalism in the wild.

Mike Driscoll has been programming in Python since 2006. He enjoys writing about Python on his blog at http://www.blog.pythonlibrary.org/. Mike has coauthored *Core Python refcard for DZone*. He recently authored *Python 101* and was a technical reviewer for the following books by Packt Publishing:

- *Python 3 Object-Oriented Programming*
- *Python 2.6 Graphics Cookbook*
- *Tkinter GUI Application Development Hotshot*

I would like to thank my beautiful wife, Evangeline, for supporting me throughout. I would also like to thank my friends and family for all their help. Also, thank you Jesus Christ for taking good care of me.

Enrique Escribano lives in Chicago and is working as a software engineer at Nokia. Although he is just 23 years old, he holds a master's of computer science degree from IIT (Chicago) and a master's of science degree in telecommunication engineering from ETSIT-UPM (Madrid). Enrique has also worked as a software engineer at KeepCoding and as a developer intern at Telefonica, SA, the most important Spanish tech company.

He is an expert in Java and Python and is proficient in using C/C++. Most of his projects involve working with cloud-based technologies, such as AWS, GAE, Hadoop, and so on. Enrique is also working on an open source research project based on security with software-defined networking (SDN) with professor Dong Jin at IIT Security Lab.

You can find more information about Enrique on his personal website at enriquescribano.com. You can also reach him on LinkedIn at linkedin.com/in/enriqueescribano.

I would like to thank my parents, Lucio and Carmen, for all the unconditional support they have provided me with over the years. They allowed me to be as ambitious as I wanted. Without them, I may never have gotten to where I am today.

I would like to thank my siblings, Francisco and Marta. Being the eldest brother is challenging, but you both keep inspiring me everyday.

Lastly, I would also like to thank Paula for always being my main inspiration and motivation since the very first day. I am so fortunate to have her in my life.

Mosudi Isiaka is a graduate in electrical and computer engineering from the Federal University of Technology Minna, Niger State, Nigeria. He demonstrates excellent skills in numerous aspects of information and communication technology. From a simple network to a mid-level complex network scenario of no less than one thousand workstations (Microsoft Windows 7, Microsoft Windows Vista, and Microsoft Windows XP), along with a Microsoft Windows 2008 Server R2 Active Directory domain controller deployed in more than a single location, Mosudi has extensive experience in implementing and managing a local area network. He has successfully set up a data center infrastructure, VPN, WAN link optimization, firewall and intrusion detection system, web/e-mail hosting control panel, OpenNMS network management application, and so on.

Mosudi has the ability to use open source software and applications to achieve enterprise-level network management solutions in scenarios that cover a virtual private network (VPN), IP PBX, cloud computing, clustering, virtualization, routing, high availability, customized firewall with advanced web filtering, network load balancing, failover and link aggregation for multiple Internet access solutions, traffic engineering, collaboration suits, network-attached storage (NAS), Linux systems administration, virtual networking and computing.

He is currently employed as a data center manager at One Network Ltd., Nigeria. Mosudi also works with ServerAfrica(http://www.serverafrica.com) as a managing consultant (technicals).

You can find more information about him at http://www.mioemi.com. You can also reach him at http://ng.linkedin.com/pub/isiaka-mosudi/1b/7a2/936/.

I would like to thank my amiable wife, Mosudi Efundayo Coker, for her moral support.

Also, many thanks to my colleague, Oyebode Micheal Tosin, for his timely reminders and technical suggestions during the reviewing process.

www.PacktPub.com

Support files, eBooks, discount offers, and more

For support files and downloads related to your book, please visit www.PacktPub.com.

Did you know that Packt offers eBook versions of every book published, with PDF and ePub files available? You can upgrade to the eBook version at www.PacktPub.com and as a print book customer, you are entitled to a discount on the eBook copy. Get in touch with us at service@packtpub.com for more details.

At www.PacktPub.com, you can also read a collection of free technical articles, sign up for a range of free newsletters and receive exclusive discounts and offers on Packt books and eBooks.

https://www2.packtpub.com/books/subscription/packtlib

Do you need instant solutions to your IT questions? PacktLib is Packt's online digital book library. Here, you can search, access, and read Packt's entire library of books.

Why subscribe?

- Fully searchable across every book published by Packt
- Copy and paste, print, and bookmark content
- On demand and accessible via a web browser

Free access for Packt account holders

If you have an account with Packt at www.PacktPub.com, you can use this to access PacktLib today and view 9 entirely free books. Simply use your login credentials for immediate access.

Table of Contents

Preface

The idea of this book came to me from the nice people at Packt Publishing. They wanted someone who could delve into the intricacies of high performance in Python and everything related to this subject, be it profiling, the available tools (such as profilers and other performance enhancement techniques), or even alternatives to the standard Python implementation.

Having said that, I welcome you to *Mastering Python High Performance*. In this book, we'll cover everything related to performance improvements. Knowledge about the subject is not strictly required (although it won't hurt), but knowledge of the Python programming language is required, especially in some of the Python-specific chapters.

We'll start by going through the basics of what profiling is, how it fits into the development cycle, and the benefits related to including this practice in it. Afterwards, we'll move on to the core tools required to get the job done (profilers and visual profilers). Then, we will take a look at a set of optimization techniques and finally arrive at a fully practical chapter that will provide a real-life optimization example.

What this book covers

Chapter 1, Profiling 101, provides information about the art of profiling to those who are not aware of it.

Chapter 2, The Profilers, tells you how to use the core tools that will be mentioned throughout the book.

Chapter 3, Going Visual – GUIs to Help Understand Profiler Output, covers how to use the pyprof2calltree and RunSnakeRun tools. It also helps the developer to understand the output of cProfile with different visualization techniques.

Chapter 4, Optimize Everything, talks about the basic process of optimization and a set of good/recommended practices that every Python developer should follow before considering other options.

Chapter 5, Multithreading versus Multiprocessing, discusses multithreading and multiprocessing and explains how and when to apply them.

Chapter 6, Generic Optimization Options, describes and shows you how to install and use Cython and PyPy in order to improve code performance.

Chapter 7, Lightning Fast Number Crunching with Numba, Parakeet, and pandas, talks about tools that help optimize Python scripts that deal with numbers. These specific tools (Numba, Parakeet, and pandas) help make number crunching faster.

Chapter 8, Putting It All into Practice, provides a practical example of profilers, finds its bottlenecks, and removes them using the tools and techniques mentioned in this book. To conclude, we'll compare the results of using each technique.

What you need for this book

Your system must have the following software before executing the code mentioned in this book:

- Python 2.7
- Line profiler 1.0b2
- Kcachegrind 0.7.4
- RunSnakeRun 2.0.4
- Numba 0.17
- The latest version of Parakeet
- pandas 0.15.2

Who this book is for

Since the topics tackled in this book cover everything related to profiling and optimizing the Python code, Python developers at all levels will benefit from this book.

The only essential requirement is to have some basic knowledge of the Python programing language.

Conventions

In this book, you will find a number of text styles that distinguish between different kinds of information. Here are some examples of these styles and an explanation of their meaning.

Code words in text, database table names, folder names, filenames, file extensions, pathnames, dummy URLs, user input, and Twitter handles are shown as follows: "We can print/gather the information we deem relevant inside the PROFILER function."

A block of code is set as follows:

```
import sys

def profiler(frame, event, arg):
    print 'PROFILER: %r %r' % (event, arg)

sys.setprofile(profiler)
```

When we wish to draw your attention to a particular part of a code block, the relevant lines or items are set in bold:

```
Traceback (most recent call last):
  File "cprof-test1.py", line 7, in <module>
    runRe() ...
  File "/usr/lib/python2.7/cProfile.py", line 140, in runctx
    exec cmd in globals, locals
  File "<string>", line 1, in <module>
NameError: name 're' is not defined
```

Any command-line input or output is written as follows:

```
$ sudo apt-get install python-dev libxml2-dev libxslt-dev
```

New terms and **important words** are shown in bold. Words that you see on the screen, for example, in menus or dialog boxes, appear in the text like this: "Again, with the **Callee Map** selected for the first function call, we can see the entire map of our script."

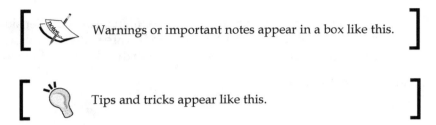

Warnings or important notes appear in a box like this.

Tips and tricks appear like this.

Reader feedback

Feedback from our readers is always welcome. Let us know what you think about this book—what you liked or disliked. Reader feedback is important for us as it helps us develop titles that you will really get the most out of.

To send us general feedback, simply e-mail feedback@packtpub.com, and mention the book's title in the subject of your message.

If there is a topic that you have expertise in and you are interested in either writing or contributing to a book, see our author guide at www.packtpub.com/authors.

Customer support

Now that you are the proud owner of a Packt book, we have a number of things to help you to get the most from your purchase.

Downloading the example code

You can download the example code files from your account at http://www.packtpub.com for all the Packt Publishing books you have purchased. If you purchased this book elsewhere, you can visit http://www.packtpub.com/support and register to have the files e-mailed directly to you.

Downloading the color images of this book

We also provide you with a PDF file that has color images of the screenshots/diagrams used in this book. The color images will help you better understand the changes in the output. You can download this file from: `https://www.packtpub.com/sites/default/files/downloads/9300OS_GraphicBundle.pdf`.

Errata

Although we have taken every care to ensure the accuracy of our content, mistakes do happen. If you find a mistake in one of our books—maybe a mistake in the text or the code—we would be grateful if you could report this to us. By doing so, you can save other readers from frustration and help us improve subsequent versions of this book. If you find any errata, please report them by visiting `http://www.packtpub.com/submit-errata`, selecting your book, clicking on the **Errata Submission Form** link, and entering the details of your errata. Once your errata are verified, your submission will be accepted and the errata will be uploaded to our website or added to any list of existing errata under the Errata section of that title.

To view the previously submitted errata, go to `https://www.packtpub.com/books/content/support` and enter the name of the book in the search field. The required information will appear under the **Errata** section.

Piracy

Piracy of copyrighted material on the Internet is an ongoing problem across all media. At Packt, we take the protection of our copyright and licenses very seriously. If you come across any illegal copies of our works in any form on the Internet, please provide us with the location address or website name immediately so that we can pursue a remedy.

Please contact us at `copyright@packtpub.com` with a link to the suspected pirated material.

We appreciate your help in protecting our authors and our ability to bring you valuable content.

Questions

If you have a problem with any aspect of this book, you can contact us at `questions@packtpub.com`, and we will do our best to address the problem.

1
Profiling 101

Just like any infant needs to learn how to crawl before running 100 mts with obstacles in under 12 seconds, programmers need to understand the basics of profiling before trying to master that art. So, before we start delving into the mysteries of performance optimization and profiling on Python programs, we need to have a clear understanding of the basics.

Once you know the basics, you'll be able to learn about the tools and techniques. So, to start us off, this chapter will cover everything you need to know about profiling but were too afraid to ask. In this chapter we will do the following things:

- We will provide a clear definition of what profiling is and the different profiling techniques.

- We will explain the importance of profiling in the development cycle, because profiling is not something you do only once and then forget about it. Profiling should be an integral part of the development process, just like writing tests is.

- We will cover things we can profile. We'll go over the different types of resources we'll be able to measure and how they'll help us find our problems.

- We will discuss the risk of premature optimization, that is, why optimizing before profiling is generally a bad idea.

- You will learn about running time complexity. Understanding profiling techniques is one step into successful optimization, but we also need to understand how to measure the complexity of an algorithm in order to understand whether we need to improve it or not.

- We will also look at good practices. Finally, we'll go over some good practices to keep in mind when starting the profiling process of your project.

What is profiling?

A program that hasn't been optimized will normally spend most of its CPU cycles in some particular subroutines. Profiling is the analysis of how the code behaves in relation to the resources it's using. For instance, profiling will tell you how much CPU time an instruction is using or how much memory the full program is consuming. It is achieved by modifying either the source code of the program or the binary executable form (when possible) to use something called as a profiler.

Normally, developers profile their programs when they need to either optimize their performance or when those programs are suffering from some kind of weird bug, which can normally be associated with memory leaks. In such cases, profiling can help them get an in-depth understanding of how their code is using the computer's resources (that is, how many times a certain function is being called).

A developer can use this information, along with a working knowledge of the source code, to find the program's bottlenecks and memory leaks. The developer can then fix whatever is wrong with the code.

There are two main methodologies for profiling software: event-based profiling and statistical profiling. When using these types of software, you should keep in mind that they both have pros and cons.

Event-based profiling

Not every programming language supports this type of profiling. Here are some programming languages that support event-based profiling:

- **Java**: The **JVMTI (JVM Tools Interface)** provides hooks for profilers to trap events such as calls, thread-related events, class loads and so on

- **.NET**: Just like with Java, the runtime provides events (http://en.wikibooks.org/wiki/Introduction_to_Software_Engineering/Testing/Profiling#Methods_of_data_gathering)

- **Python**: Using the `sys.setprofile` function, a developer can trap events such as `python_[call|return|exception]` or `c_[call|return|exception]`

Event-based profilers (also known as **tracing profilers**) work by gathering data on specific events during the execution of our program. These profilers generate a large amount of data. Basically, the more events they listen to, the more data they will gather. This makes them somewhat impractical to use, and they are not the first choice when starting to profile a program. However, they are a good last resort when other profiling methods aren't enough or just aren't specific enough. Consider the case where you'd want to profile all the return statements. This type of profiler would give you the granularity you'd need for this task, while others would simply not allow you to execute this task.

A simple example of an event-based profiler on Python could be the following code (we'll understand this topic better once we reach the upcoming chapters):

```python
import sys

def profiler(frame, event, arg):
    print 'PROFILER: %r %r' % (event, arg)

sys.setprofile(profiler)

#simple (and very ineficient) example of how to calculate the
Fibonacci sequence for a number.
def fib(n):
    if n == 0:
        return 0
    elif n == 1:
        return 1
    else:
        return fib(n-1) + fib(n-2)

def fib_seq(n):
    seq = [ ]
    if n > 0:
        seq.extend(fib_seq(n-1))
    seq.append(fib(n))
    return seq

print fib_seq(2)
```

The preceding code contributes to the following output:

```
PROFILER: 'call' None
PROFILER: 'call' None
PROFILER: 'call' None
PROFILER: 'call' None
PROFILER: 'return' 0
PROFILER: 'c_call' <built-in method append of list object at
0x7f570ca215f0>
PROFILER: 'c_return' <built-in method append of list object at
0x7f570ca215f0>
PROFILER: 'return' [0]
PROFILER: 'c_call' <built-in method extend of list object at
0x7f570ca21bd8>
PROFILER: 'c_return' <built-in method extend of list object at
0x7f570ca21bd8>
PROFILER: 'call' None
PROFILER: 'return' 1
PROFILER: 'c_call' <built-in method append of list object at
0x7f570ca21bd8>
PROFILER: 'c_return' <built-in method append of list object at
0x7f570ca21bd8>
PROFILER: 'return' [0, 1]
PROFILER: 'c_call' <built-in method extend of list object at
0x7f570ca55bd8>
PROFILER: 'c_return' <built-in method extend of list object at
0x7f570ca55bd8>
PROFILER: 'call' None
PROFILER: 'call' None
PROFILER: 'return' 1
PROFILER: 'call' None
PROFILER: 'return' 0
PROFILER: 'return' 1
PROFILER: 'c_call' <built-in method append of list object at
0x7f570ca55bd8>
PROFILER: 'c_return' <built-in method append of list object at
0x7f570ca55bd8>
PROFILER: 'return' [0, 1, 1]
[0, 1, 1]
PROFILER: 'return' None
PROFILER: 'call' None
PROFILER: 'c_call' <built-in method discard of set object at
0x7f570ca8a960>
PROFILER: 'c_return' <built-in method discard of set object at
0x7f570ca8a960>
PROFILER: 'return' None
```

```
PROFILER: 'call' None
PROFILER: 'c_call' <built-in method discard of set object at
0x7f570ca8f3f0>
PROFILER: 'c_return' <built-in method discard of set object at
0x7f570ca8f3f0>
PROFILER: 'return' None
```

As you can see, PROFILER is called on every event. We can print/gather the information we deem relevant inside the PROFILER function. The last line on the sample code shows that the simple execution of fib_seq(2) generates a lot of output data. If we were dealing with a real-world program, this output would be several orders of magnitude bigger. This is why event-based profiling is normally the last option when it comes to profiling. There are other alternatives out there (as we'll see) that generate much less output, but, of course, have a lower accuracy rate.

Statistical profiling

Statistical profilers work by sampling the program counter at regular intervals. This in turn allows the developer to get an idea of how much time the target program is spending on each function. Since it works by sampling the PC, the resulting numbers will be a statistical approximation of reality instead of exact numbers. Still, it should be enough to get a glimpse of what the profiled program is doing and where the bottlenecks are.

Some advantages of this type of profiling are as follows:

- **Less data to analyze**: Since we're only sampling the program's execution instead of saving every little piece of data, the amount of information to analyze will be significantly smaller.

- **Smaller profiling footprint**: Due to the way the sampling is made (using OS interrupts), the target program suffers a smaller hit on its performance. Although the presence of the profiler is not 100 percent unnoticed, statistical profiling does less damage than the event-based one.

Here is an example of the output of **OProfile** (http://oprofile.sourceforge.net/news/), a Linux statistical profiler:

```
Function name,File name,Times Encountered,Percentage
"func80000","statistical_profiling.c",30760,48.96%
"func40000","statistical_profiling.c",17515,27.88%
"func20000","static_functions.c",7141,11.37%
"func10000","static_functions.c",3572,5.69%
"func5000","static_functions.c",1787,2.84%
"func2000","static_functions.c",768,1.22%
```

```
"func1500","statistical_profiling.c",701,1.12%
"func1000","static_functions.c",385,0.61%
"func500","statistical_profiling.c",194,0.31%
```

Here is the output of profiling the same Fibonacci code from the preceding code using a statistical profiler for Python called statprof:

```
  %    cumulative    self
 time    seconds    seconds  name
100.00     0.01       0.01    B02088_01_03.py:11:fib
  0.00     0.01       0.00    B02088_01_03.py:17:fib_seq
  0.00     0.01       0.00    B02088_01_03.py:21:<module>
---
Sample count: 1
Total time: 0.010000 seconds
```

As you can see, there is quite a difference between the output of both profilers for the same code.

The importance of profiling

Now that we know what profiling means, it is also important to understand how important and relevant it is to actually do it during the development cycle of our applications.

Profiling is not something everyone is used to do, especially with non-critical software (unlike peace maker embedded software or any other type of execution-critical example). Profiling takes time and is normally useful only after we've detected that something is wrong with our program. However, it could still be performed before that even happens to catch possible unseen bugs, which would, in turn, help chip away the time spent debugging the application at a later stage.

As hardware keeps advancing, getting faster and cheaper, it is increasingly hard to understand why we, as developers, should spend resources (mainly time) on profiling our creations. After all, we have practices such as test-driven development, code review, pair programming and others that assure us our code is solid and that it'll work as we want it. Right?

However, what we sometimes fail to realize is that the higher level our languages become (we've gone from assembler to JavaScript in just a few years), the less we think about CPU cycles, memory allocation, CPU registers, and so on. New generations of programmers learn their craft using higher level languages because they're easier to understand and provide more power out of the box. However, they also abstract the hardware and our interaction with it. As this tendency keeps growing, the chances that new developers will even consider profiling their software as another step on its development grows weaker by the second.

Let's look at the following scenario:

As we know, profiling measures the resources our program uses. As I've stated earlier, they keep getting cheaper and cheaper. So, the cost of getting our software out and the cost of making it available to a higher number of users is also getting cheaper.

These days, it is increasingly easy to create and publish an application that will be reached by thousands of people. If they like it and spread the word through social media, that number can blow up exponentially. Once that happens, something that is very common is that the software will crash, or it'll become impossibly slow and the users will just go away.

A possible explanation for the preceding scenario is, of course, a badly thought and non-scalable architecture. After all, one single server with a limited amount of RAM and processing power will get you so far until it becomes your bottleneck. However, another possible explanation, one that proves to be true many times, is that we failed to stress test our application. We didn't think about resource consumption; we just made sure our tests passed, and we were happy with that. In other words, we failed to go that extra mile, and as a result, our project crashed and burned.

Profiling can help avoid that crash and burn outcome, since it provides a fairly accurate view of what our program is doing, no matter the load. So, if we profile it with a very light load, and the result is that we're spending 80 percent of our time doing some kind of I/O operation, it might raise a flag for us. Even if, during our test, the application performed correctly, it might not do so under heavy stress. Think of a memory leak-type scenario. In those cases, small tests might not generate a big enough problem for us to detect it. However, a production deployment under heavy stress will. Profiling can provide enough evidence for us to detect this problem before it even turns into one.

What can we profile?

Going deeper into profiling, it is very important to understand what we can actually profile. Measuring is the core of profiling, so let's take a detailed look at the things we can measure during a program's execution.

Execution time

The most basic of the numbers we can gather when profiling is the execution time. The execution time of the entire process or just of a particular portion of the code will shed some light on its own. If you have experience in the area your program is running (that is, you're a web developer and you're working on a web framework), you probably already know what it means for your system to take too much time. For instance, a simple web server might take up to 100 milliseconds when querying the database, rendering the response, and sending it back to the client. However, if the same piece of code starts to slow down and now it takes 60 seconds to do the same task, then you should start thinking about profiling. You also have to consider that numbers here are relative. Let's assume another process: a MapReduce job that is meant to process 2 TB of information stored on a set of text files takes 20 minutes. In this case, you might not consider it as a slow process, even when it takes considerably more time than the slow web server mentioned earlier.

To get this type of information, you don't really need a lot of profiling experience or even complex tools to get the numbers. Just add the required lines into your code and run the program.

For instance, the following code will calculate the Fibonnacci sequence for the number 30:

```python
import datetime

tstart = None
tend = None

def start_time():
    global tstart
    tstart = datetime.datetime.now()
def get_delta():
    global tstart
    tend = datetime.datetime.now()
    return tend - tstart


def fib(n):
```

```
        return n if n == 0 or n == 1 else fib(n-1) + fib(n-2)

    def fib_seq(n):
        seq = [ ]
        if n > 0:
            seq.extend(fib_seq(n-1))
        seq.append(fib(n))
        return seq

    start_time()
    print "About to calculate the fibonacci sequence for the number 30"
    delta1 = get_delta()

    start_time()
    seq = fib_seq(30)
    delta2 = get_delta()

    print "Now we print the numbers: "
    start_time()
    for n in seq:
        print n
    delta3 = get_delta()

    print "====== Profiling results ======="
    print "Time required to print a simple message: %(delta1)s" % locals()
    print "Time required to calculate fibonacci: %(delta2)s" % locals()
    print "Time required to iterate and print the numbers: %(delta3)s" %
    locals()
    print "======   ======="
```

Now, the code will produce the following output:

```
About to calculate the Fibonacci sequence for the number 30
Now we print the numbers:
0
1
1
2
3
5
8
13
21
#...more numbers
4181
```

```
6765
10946
17711
28657
46368
75025
121393
196418
317811
514229
832040
====== Profiling results =======
Time required to print a simple message: 0:00:00.000030
Time required to calculate fibonacci: 0:00:00.642092
Time required to iterate and print the numbers: 0:00:00.000102
```

Based on the last three lines, we see the obvious results: the most expensive part of the code is the actual calculation of the Fibonacci sequence.

> **Downloading the example code**
>
> You can download the example code files from your account at
> http://www.packtpub.com for all the Packt Publishing books
> you have purchased. If you purchased this book elsewhere, you
> can visit http://www.packtpub.com/support and register
> to have the files e-mailed directly to you.

Where are the bottlenecks?

Once you've measured how much time your code needs to execute, you can profile it by paying special attention to the slow sections. These are the bottlenecks, and normally, they are related to one or a combination of the following reasons:

- Heavy I/O operations, such as reading and parsing big files, executing long-running database queries, calling external services (such as HTTP requests), and so on

- Unexpected memory leaks that start building up until there is no memory left for the rest of the program to execute properly

- Unoptimized code that gets executed frequently

- Intensive operations that are not cached when they could be

I/O-bound code (file reads/write, database queries, and so on) is usually harder to optimize, because that would imply changing the way the program is dealing with that I/O (normally using core functions from the language). Instead, when optimizing compute-bound code (like a function that is using a badly implemented algorithm), getting a performance improvement is easier (although not necessarily easy). This is because it just implies rewriting it.

A general indicator that you're near the end of a performance optimization process is when most of the bottlenecks left are due to I/O-bound code.

Memory consumption and memory leaks

Another very important resource to consider when developing software is memory. Regular software developers don't really care much about it, since the era of the 640 KB of RAM PC is long dead. However, a memory leak on a long-running program can turn any server into a 640 KB computer. Memory consumption is not just about having enough memory for your program to run; it's also about having control over the memory that your programs use.

There are some developments, such as embedded systems, that actually require developers to pay extra attention to the amount of memory they use, because it is a limited resource in those systems. However, an average developer can expect their target system to have the amount of RAM they require.

With RAM and higher level languages that come with automatic memory management (like garbage collection), the developer is less likely to pay much attention to memory utilization, trusting the platform to do it for them.

Keeping track of memory consumption is relatively straightforward. At least for a basic approach, just use your OS's task manager. It'll display, among other things, the amount of memory used or at least the percentage of total memory used by your program. The task manager is also a great tool to check your CPU time consumption. As you can see in the next screenshot, a simple Python program (the preceding one) is taking up almost the entire CPU power (99.8 percent), and barely 0.1 percent of the total memory that is available:

```
Activities                                                              Wed 23:48

top - 23:48:31 up 7 days, 14:22,  1 user,  load average: 0.63, 0.48, 0.44
Tasks: 316 total,   2 running, 313 sleeping,   1 stopped,   0 zombie
%Cpu(s): 15.2 us,  0.8 sy,  0.0 ni, 78.3 id,  5.8 wa,  0.0 hi,  0.0 si,  0.0 st
KiB Mem:   7945412 total,  7722940 used,   222472 free,    27616 buffers
KiB Swap:  8155132 total,  2503856 used,  5651276 free.  1587528 cached Mem

  PID USER      PR  NI    VIRT    RES    SHR S  %CPU %MEM     TIME+ COMMAND
12469 fernando  20   0   40228   5564   2140 R 100.0  0.1   0:04.22 python
 3661 fernando  20   0 2124352 252696  21332 S   9.0  3.2  83:27.11 gnome-shell
 2585 root      20   0  873972 230080 198948 S   5.3  2.9  61:26.63 Xorg
 4483 fernando  20   0 3210628 1.328g  24340 S   5.3 17.5 414:52.19 firefox
 4193 fernando  20   0  792124  91796  15036 S   2.7  1.2  98:23.23 skype
10458 fernando  20   0 1041804 305700  67784 S   2.3  3.8   7:43.42 chrome
 4073 fernando  20   0  771384  19284   6372 S   1.3  0.2 129:36.18 chrome
 3541 fernando  20   0  396220  47876   1248 S   0.7  0.6   7:34.36 ibus-daemon
 4049 fernando  20   0  771384  19156   6308 S   0.7  0.2 129:06.05 chrome
 3625 fernando  20   0  200952   1232    696 S   0.3  0.0   1:19.11 ibus-engine-sim
 3640 fernando  20   0  446296   4412   2576 S   0.3  0.1  83:21.54 pulseaudio
 3742 fernando  20   0  781660  11172   5616 S   0.3  0.1   0:58.55 guake
 3985 fernando  20   0 2053884 304428  41080 S   0.3  3.8 144:36.67 chrome
 4027 fernando  20   0 2772532 618964 124452 S   0.3  7.8  54:11.44 chrome
 4685 fernando  20   0  957004  48140   4028 S   0.3  0.6  70:33.78 plugin-containe
 4729 fernando  20   0  585360   2668   1412 S   0.3  0.0   8:43.31 GoogleTalkPlugi
11031 fernando  20   0  703200  25092   7212 S   0.3  0.3   0:23.71 chrome
    1 root      20   0   34012   2352    800 S   0.0  0.0   0:02.65 init
    2 root      20   0       0      0      0 S   0.0  0.0   0:00.10 kthreadd
    3 root      20   0       0      0      0 S   0.0  0.0   0:00.57 ksoftirqd/0
    5 root       0 -20       0      0      0 S   0.0  0.0   0:00.00 kworker/0:0H
    7 root      20   0       0      0      0 S   0.0  0.0   2:44.79 rcu_sched
    8 root      20   0       0      0      0 S   0.0  0.0   1:06.13 rcuos/0
    9 root      20   0       0      0      0 S   0.0  0.0   0:25.07 rcuos/1
   10 root      20   0       0      0      0 S   0.0  0.0   1:02.09 rcuos/2
   11 root      20   0       0      0      0 S   0.0  0.0   0:23.90 rcuos/3
   12 root      20   0       0      0      0 S   0.0  0.0   0:53.74 rcuos/4
   13 root      20   0       0      0      0 S   0.0  0.0   0:21.49 rcuos/5
   14 root      20   0       0      0      0 S   0.0  0.0   0:43.98 rcuos/6
   15 root      20   0       0      0      0 S   0.0  0.0   0:27.86 rcuos/7
   16 root      20   0       0      0      0 S   0.0  0.0   0:00.00 rcu_bh
   17 root      20   0       0      0      0 S   0.0  0.0   0:00.00 rcuob/0
```

With a tool like that (the `top` command line tool from Linux), spotting memory leaks can be easy, but that will depend on the type of software you're monitoring. If your program is constantly loading data, its memory consumption rate will be different from another program that doesn't have to deal much with external resources.

For instance, if we were to chart the memory consumption over time of a program dealing with lots of external data, it would look like the following chart:

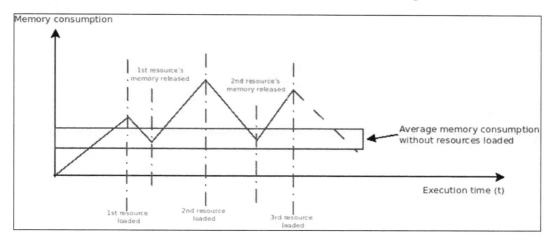

There will be peaks, when these resources get fully loaded into memory, but there will also be some drops, when those resources are released. Although the memory consumption numbers fluctuate quite a bit, it's still possible to estimate the average amount of memory that the program will use when no resources are loaded. Once you define that area (marked as a green box in the preceding chart), you can spot memory leaks.

Let's look at how the same chart would look with bad resource handling (not fully releasing allocated memory):

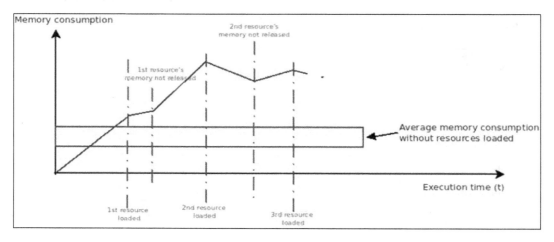

In the preceding chart, you can clearly see that not all memory is released when a resource is no longer used, which is causing the line to move out of the green box. This means the program is consuming more and more memory every second, even when the resources loaded are released.

The same can be done with programs that aren't resource heavy, for instance, scripts that execute a particular processing task for a considerable period of time. In those cases, the memory consumption and the leaks should be easier to spot.

Let's take a look at an example:

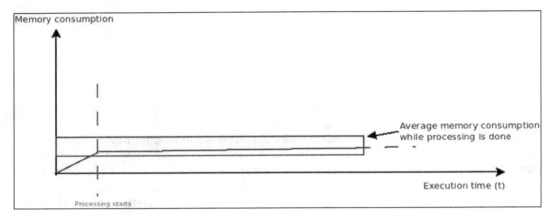

When the processing stage starts, the memory consumption should stabilize within a clearly defined range. If we spot numbers outside that range, especially if it goes out of it and never comes back, we're looking at another example of a memory leak.

Let's look at an example of such a case:

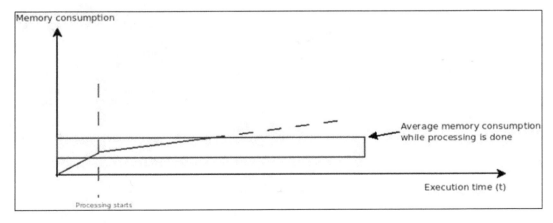

The risk of premature optimization

Optimization is normally considered a good practice. However, this doesn't hold true when the act of optimization ends up driving the design decisions of the software solution.

A very common pitfall developers face while starting to code a new piece of software is premature optimization.

When this happens, the end result ends up being quite the opposite of the intended optimized code. It can contain an incomplete version of the required solution, or it can even contain errors derived from the optimization-driven design decisions.

As a normal rule of thumb, if you haven't measured (profiled) your code, optimizing it might not be the best idea. First, focus on readable code. Then, profile it and find out where the real bottlenecks are, and as a final step, perform the actual optimization.

Running time complexity

When profiling and optimizing code, it's really important to understand what **Running time complexity (RTC)** is and how we can use that knowledge to properly optimize our code.

RTC helps quantify the execution time of a given algorithm. It does so by providing a mathematical approximation of the time a piece of code will take to execute for any given input. It is an approximation, because that way, we're able to group similar algorithms using that value.

RTC is expressed using something called **Big O notation**. In mathematics, Big O notation is used to express the limiting behavior of a given function when the terms tend to infinity. If I apply that concept in computer science, we can use Big O notation to express the limiting behavior of the function describing the execution time.

In other words, this notation will give us a broad idea of how long our algorithm will take to process an arbitrarily large input. It will not, however, give us a precise number for the time of execution, which would require a more in-depth analysis of the source code.

As I've said earlier, we can use this tendency to group algorithms. Here are some of the most common groups:

Constant time – O(1)

This is the simplest of them all. This notation basically means that the action we're measuring will always take a constant amount of time, and this time is not dependent on the size of the input.

Here are some examples of code that have *O(1)* execution time:

- Determining whether a number is odd or even:

```
if number % 2:
    odd = True
else:
    odd = False
```

- Printing a message into standard output:

```
print "Hello world!"
```

Even something more conceptually complex, like finding the value of a key inside a dictionary (or hash table), if implemented correctly, can be done in constant time. Technically speaking, accessing an element on the hash takes *O(1)* amortized time, which roughly means that the average time each operation takes (without taking into account edge cases) is a constant *O(1)* time.

Linear time – O(n)

Linear time dictates that for a given input of arbitrary length n, the amount of time required for the execution of the algorithm is linearly proportional to n, for instance, $3n$, $4n + 5$, and so on.

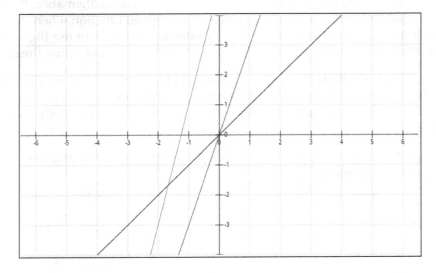

The preceding chart clearly shows that both the blue (*3n*) line and the red one (*4n + 5*) have the same upper limit as the black line (*n*) when *x* tends to infinity. So, to simplify, we can just say that all three functions are *O(n)*.

Examples of algorithms with this execution order are:

- Finding the smallest value in an unsorted list
- Comparing two strings
- Deleting the last item inside a linked list

Logarithmic time – O(log n)

An algorithm with logarithmic execution time is one that will have a very determined upper limit time. A logarithmic function grows quickly at first, but it'll slow down as the input size gets bigger. It will never stop growing, but the amount it grows by will be so small that it will be irrelevant.

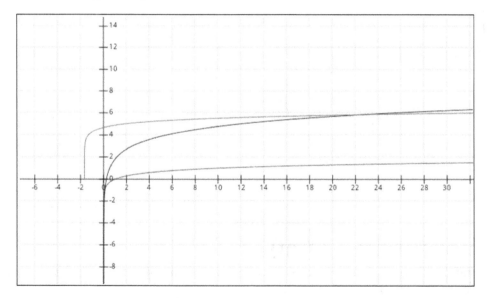

The preceding chart shows three different logarithmic functions. You can clearly see that they all possess a similar shape, including the upper limit *x*, which keeps increasing to infinity.

Some examples of algorithms that have logarithmic execution time are:

- Binary search
- Calculating Fibonacci numbers (using matrix multiplications)

Linearithmic time – O(nlog n)

A particular combination of the previous two orders of execution is the linearithmic time. It grows quickly as soon as the value of *x* starts increasing.

Here are some examples of algorithms that have this order of execution:

- Merge sort
- Heap sort
- Quick sort (at least its average time complexity)

Let's see a few examples of plotted linearithmic functions to understand them better:

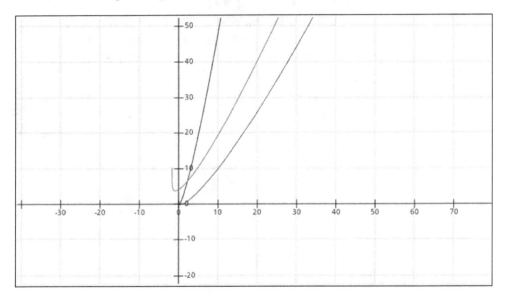

Factorial time – O(n!)

Factorial time is one of the worst execution times we might get out of an algorithm. It grows so quickly that it's hard to plot.

Here is a rough approximation of how the execution time of our algorithm would look with factorial time:

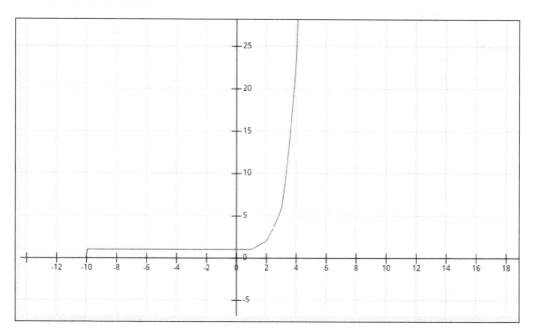

An example of an algorithm with factorial execution time is the solution for the traveling salesman using brute force search (basically checking every single possible solution).

Quadratic time – O(n^)

Quadratic execution time is another example of a fast growing algorithm. The bigger the input size, the longer it's going to take (this is true for most complexities, but then again, specially true for this one). Quadratic execution time is even less efficient that linearithmic time.

Some examples of algorithms having this order of execution are:

- Bubble sort
- Traversing a 2D array
- Insertion sort

Here are some examples of plotted exponential functions:

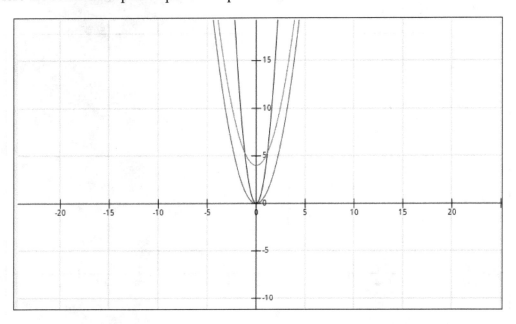

Finally, let's look at all examples plotted together to get a clear idea of algorithm efficiency:

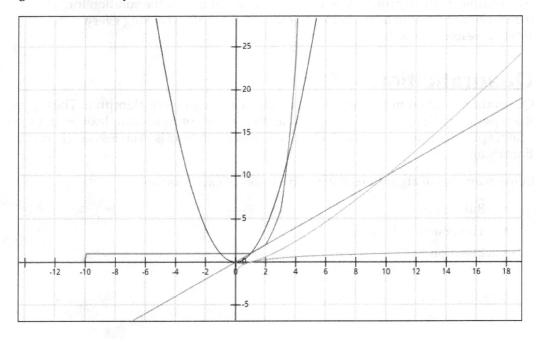

Leaving aside constant execution time, which is clearly faster but most of the time impossible to achieve in complex algorithms, the order or preference should be:

- Logarithmic
- Linear
- Linearithmic
- Quadratic
- Factorial

Obviously, there are cases when you'll have no choice but to get a quadratic execution time as the best possible result. The idea is to always aim for the faster algorithms, but the limitations of your problems and technology will affect the actual result.

 Note that between quadratic and factorial times, there are several other alternatives (cubic, $n \wedge 4$, and so on).

Another important consideration is that most algorithms don't have only a single order of execution time. They can have up to three orders of execution time: for the best case, normal case, and worst case scenarios. The scenario is determined by the properties of the input data. For instance, the insertion sort algorithm will run much faster if the input is already sorted (best case), and it will be worst (exponential order) for other types of input.

Other interesting cases to look at are the data types used. They inherently come with execution time that is associated with actions you can perform on them (lookup, insert, search, and so on). Let's look at some of the most common data types and their associated actions:

Data Structure	Time complexity							
	Average case				Worst case			
	Indexing	Search	Insertion	Deletion	Indexing	Search	Insertion	Deletion
List	$O(1)$	$O(n)$	-	-	$O(1)$	$O(n)$	-	-
Linked list	$O(n)$	$O(n)$	$O(1)$	$O(1)$	$O(n)$	$O(n)$	$O(1)$	$O(n)$
Doubly linked list	$O(n)$	$O(n)$	$O(1)$	$O(1)$	$O(n)$	$O(n)$	$O(1)$	$O(1)$
Dictionary	-	$O(1)$	$O(1)$	$O(1)$	-	$O(n)$	$O(n)$	$O(n)$
Binary search tree	$O(log(n))$	$O(log(n))$	$O(log(n))$	$O(log(n))$	$O(n)$	$O(n)$	$O(n)$	$O(n)$

Profiling best practices

Profiling is a repetitive task. You'll do it several times inside the same project in order to get the best results, and you'll do it again on the next project. Just like with any other repetitive task in software development, there is a set of best practices you can follow to ensure that you get the most out of the process. Let's look at some of them:

Build a regression-test suite

Before starting any kind of optimization process, you need to make sure that the changes you make to the code will not affect its functioning in a bad way. The best way to do this, especially when it's a big code base, is to create a test suite. Make sure that your code coverage is high enough to provide the confidence you need to make the changes. A test suite with 60 percent code coverage can lead to very bad results.

A regression-test suite will allow you to make as many optimization tries as you need to without fear of breaking the code.

Mind your code

Functional code tends to be easier to refactor, mainly because the functions structured that way tend to avoid side effects. This reduces any risk of affecting unwanted parts of your system. If your functions avoid a local mutable state, that's another winning point for you. This is because the code should be pretty straightforward for you to understand and change. Functions that don't follow the previously mentioned guidelines will require more work and care while refactoring.

Be patient

Profiling is not fast, not easy, and not an exact process. What this means is that you should not expect to just run the profiler and expect the data from it to point directly to your problem. That could happen, yes. However, most of the time, the problems you're trying to solve are the ones that simple debugging couldn't fix. This means you'll be browsing through data, plotting it to try to make sense of it, and narrowing down the source of your problem until you either need to start again, or you find it.

Keep in mind that the deeper you get into the profiled data, the deeper into the rabbit hole you get. Numbers will stop making sense right away, so make sure you know what you're doing and that you have the right tools for the job before you start. Otherwise, you'll waste your time and end up with nothing but frustration.

Gather as much data as you can

Depending on the type and size of software you're dealing with, you might want to get as much data as you can before you start analyzing it. Profilers are a great source for this. However, there are other sources, such as server logs from web applications, custom logs, system resources snapshots (like from the OS task manager), and so on.

Preprocess your data

After you have all the information from your profilers, your logs, and other sources, you will probably need to preprocess the data before analyzing it. Don't shy away from unstructured data just because a profiler can't understand it. Your analysis of the data will benefit from the extra numbers.

For instance, getting the web server logs is a great idea if you're profiling a web application, but those files are normally just text files with one line per request. By parsing it and getting the data into some kind of database system (like MongoDB, MySQL, or the like), you'll be able to give that data meaning (by parsing the dates, doing geolocation by source IP address, and so on) and query that information afterwards.

The formal name for the stage is ETL, which stands for *extracting the data from it's sources, transforming it into something with meaning, and loading it into another system that you can later query.*

Visualize your data

If you don't know exactly what it is that you're looking for and you're just looking for ways to optimize your code before something goes wrong, a great idea to get some insight into the data you've already preprocessed is to visualize it. Computers are great with numbers, but humans, on the other hand, are great with images when we want to find patterns and understand what kind of insight we can gather from the information we have.

For instance, to continue with the web server logs example, a simple plot (such as the ones you can do with MS Excel) for the requests by hour can provide some insight into the behavior of your users:

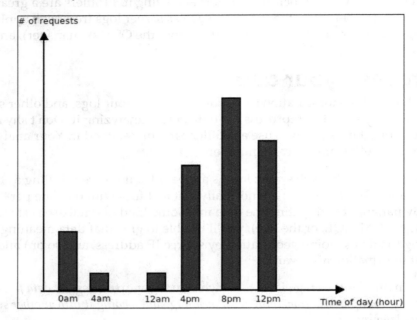

The preceding chart clearly shows that the majority of requests are done during late afternoon and continue into the night. You can use this insight later on for further profiling. For instance, an optional improvement of your setup here would be to provide more resources for your infrastructure during that time (something that can be done with service providers such as Amazon Web Services).

Another example, using custom profiling data, could be the following chart:

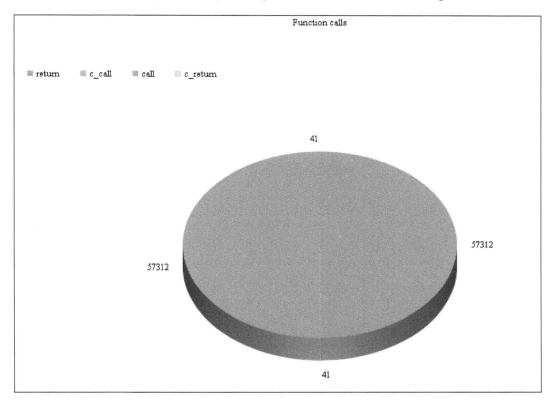

It uses data from the first code example of this chapter by counting the number of each event that triggers the profile function. We can then plot it and get an idea of the most common events. In our case, the call and return events are definitely taking up most of our program's time.

Summary

In this chapter, we've covered the basics of profiling. You understood profiling and its importance. You also learned how we can leverage it in order to get the most out of our code.

In the next chapter, we'll start getting our hands dirty by looking at some Python profilers and how we can use them on our applications.

2
The Profilers

In the previous chapter, we covered the basics of profiling and understood its importance. You learned how it will help the development process if we incorporate the practice of profiling into the cycle of development. We also went over some good profiling practices.

Finally, we covered some theory about the different execution times our program can have. In this chapter, we'll use the first part (the part about profiling). Then, with the help of two specific Python profilers (cProfile and line_profilers), we'll start putting into practice some theory that you have learned.

In this chapter, we will cover the following topics:

- Some basic information about each profiler
- How to download and install each profiler
- Use cases examples with different options
- Differences and similarities between both profilers

Getting to know our new best friends: the profilers

After all the theory and generic examples from the previous chapter, it is time for some real Python. So, let's begin with two of the most known and used Python profilers: cProfile and line_profiler. They will help us profile our code in two different ways.

On one hand, we have `cProfile` (`https://docs.python.org/2/library/profile.html#module-cProfile`), It comes by default with Python since version 2.5 and is the recommended profiler for most use cases. At least that is what the official Python documentation says about it. On the other hand, we have `line_profiler` (`https://github.com/rkern/line_profiler`), which is not an official part of the Python programming language, but it's a well-known profiler out there.

Let's go over both of them in more detail.

cProfile

Like I've already mentioned, `cProfile` comes by default with the standard Python interpreter (`cPython`) since version 2.5. Other versions, such as PyPy, don't have it. It is a deterministic profiler. It provides a set of APIs that allow the developers to gather information about the execution of Python programs, more specifically, about the CPU time used by each function. It also provides other details, such as the number of times a function was called.

It exclusively measures CPU time and pays no attention to memory consumption and other memory related stats. Nonetheless, it is a great starter point, since most of the times, if we're trying to optimize code, this type of analysis will provide an immediate set of optimization candidates.

There is no need for installation, since it's part of the language already. To use it, all you have to do is to import the `cProfile` package.

 A deterministic profiler is just another name for an event-based profiler (check out the previous chapter for more details). This means that that this profiler will be aware of every function call, return statement, and other events during the execution of our code. It will also measure everything that happens during that time (unlike the statistical profiler we saw in the previous chapter).

Here is a very simple example taken from Python's documentation:

```
import cProfile
import re
cProfile.run('re.compile("foo|bar")')
```

The preceding code outputs the following text:

```
197 function calls (192 primitive calls) in 0.002 seconds

Ordered by: standard name

ncalls  tottime  percall  cumtime  percall filename:lineno(function)
     1    0.000    0.000    0.001    0.001 <string>:1(<module>)
     1    0.000    0.000    0.001    0.001 re.py:212(compile)
     1    0.000    0.000    0.001    0.001 re.py:268(_compile)
     1    0.000    0.000    0.000    0.000
  sre_compile.py:172(_compile_charset)
     1    0.000    0.000    0.000    0.000
  sre_compile.py:201(_optimize_charset)
     4    0.000    0.000    0.000    0.000
  sre_compile.py:25(_identityfunction)
   3/1    0.000    0.000    0.000    0.000
  sre_compile.py:33(_compile)
```

From this output, the following information can be gathered:

- The first line tells us that 197 function calls were monitored, and out of them, 192 were primitive calls, which means no recursion was involved.

- ncalls reports the number of calls to the function. If there are two numbers in this column, it means there was recursion. The second one is the number of primitive calls, and the first one is the total number of calls. This number can be helpful to identify the possible bugs (unexpected high numbers) or possible inline expansion points.

- tottime is the total time spent inside the function (excluding the time spent doing subcalls to other functions). This particular information can help the developer find long running loops that could be optimized.

- percall is simply the quotient of tottime divided by ncalls.

- cumtime is the cumulative time spent inside the function including the time spent in subfunctions (this includes recursive calls as well). This number could help identify higher level errors, such as those in the selection of the algorithm.

- percall is the quotient of cumtime divided by primitive calls.

- filename:lineno(function) provides the file name, line number, and function name of the analyzed function.

A note about limitations

There is no such thing as the invisible profiler. This means that even in the case of cProfile, which has a very small overhead, it still adds an overhead to our code. On every event that is triggered, there is some lag between the time that the event actually happens and that time that the profiler gets to query the state of the internal clock. At the same time, there is some lag between the moment the program counter leaves the profiler's code and goes back into the user's code to continue with the execution.

Adding to the fact, that as any piece of data inside a computer, the internal clock has a set precision, and any measurement that is smaller than that precision will be lost. That being said, the developer needs to have a special consideration when profiling code with a high number of recursive calls or, in particular cases, when a function calls many other functions, since that error can accumulate and begin to be significant.

The API provided

The cProfile profiler provides a set of methods that will help the developer gather statistics in different contexts:

```
run(command, filename=None, sort=-1)
```

This classic method used in the preceding example gathers statistics about the execution of the command. After that, it calls the following function:

```
exec(command, __main__.__dict__, __main__.__dict__)
```

If no file name is given, it'll create a new instance of stats (more on this class in a minute). Here is the preceding same example, but using the extra parameters:

```
import cProfile
import re
cProfile.run('re.compile("foo|bar")', 'stats', 'cumtime')
```

If you run the preceding code, you'll notice that nothing gets printed out. However, if you inspect the content of the folder, you'll notice a new file, called stats. If you try to open that file, you won't be able to understand its meaning because it was saved using a binary format. In a few minutes, we'll see how to read that information and manipulate it to create our own reports:

```
runctx(command, globals, locals, filename=None)
```

This method is very similar to the preceding one. The only difference is that it also receives the `globals` and `locals` dictionaries for the command-line string. After that, it executes the following function:

```
exec(command, globals, locals)
```

It gathers profiling statistics just like `run` does. Let's see an example of the main difference between `run` and `runctx`.

Let's stick to `run` and write the following code:

```
import cProfile
def runRe():
    import re
    cProfile.run('re.compile("foo|bar")')
runRe()
```

What we would actually get when running the code is the following error message:

```
Traceback (most recent call last):
  File "cprof-test1.py", line 7, in <module>
    runRe() ...
  File "/usr/lib/python2.7/cProfile.py", line 140, in runctx
    exec cmd in globals, locals
  File "<string>", line 1, in <module>
NameError: name 're' is not defined
```

The `re` module is not found by the `run` method because as we saw earlier that `run` calls the `exec` function with the `__main__.__dict__` as parameters.

Now, let's use `runctx` in the following manner:

```
import cProfile
def runRe():
    import re
    cProfile.runctx('re.compile("foo|bar")', None, locals())
runRe()
```

Then the output would change into a valid one as follows:

```
        194 function calls (189 primitive calls) in 0.000 seconds
  Ordered by: standard name
  ncalls  tottime  percall  cumtime  percall filename:lineno(function)
       1    0.000    0.000    0.000    0.000 <string>:1(<module>)
       1    0.000    0.000    0.000    0.000 re.py:188(compile)
       1    0.000    0.000    0.000    0.000 re.py:226(_compile)
```

```
     1    0.000    0.000    0.000    0.000
   sre_compile.py:178(_compile_charset)
     1    0.000    0.000    0.000    0.000
   sre_compile.py:207(_optimize_charset)
     4    0.000    0.000    0.000    0.000
   sre_compile.py:24(_identityfunction)
   3/1    0.000    0.000    0.000    0.000
   sre_compile.py:32(_compile)
     1    0.000    0.000    0.000    0.000
   sre_compile.py:359(_compile_info)
     2    0.000    0.000    0.000    0.000
   sre_compile.py:472(isstring)
     1    0.000    0.000    0.000    0.000
   sre_compile.py:478(_code)
     1    0.000    0.000    0.000    0.000
   sre_compile.py:493(compile)
     5    0.000    0.000    0.000    0.000
   sre_parse.py:126(__len__)
    12    0.000    0.000    0.000    0.000
   sre_parse.py:130(__getitem__)
     7    0.000    0.000    0.000    0.000
   sre_parse.py:138(append)
   3/1    0.000    0.000    0.000    0.000
   sre_parse.py:140(getwidth)
     1    0.000    0.000    0.000    0.000
   sre_parse.py:178(__init__)
    10    0.000    0.000    0.000    0.000
   sre_parse.py:182(__next)
     2    0.000    0.000    0.000    0.000
   sre_parse.py:195(match)
     8    0.000    0.000    0.000    0.000
   sre_parse.py:201(get)
     1    0.000    0.000    0.000    0.000
   sre_parse.py:301(_parse_sub)
     2    0.000    0.000    0.000    0.000
   sre_parse.py:379(_parse)
     1    0.000    0.000    0.000    0.000
   sre_parse.py:67(__init__)
     1    0.000    0.000    0.000    0.000
   sre_parse.py:675(parse)
     3    0.000    0.000    0.000    0.000
   sre_parse.py:90(__init__)
     1    0.000    0.000    0.000    0.000 {_sre.compile}
    15    0.000    0.000    0.000    0.000 {isinstance}
 38/37    0.000    0.000    0.000    0.000 {len}
     2    0.000    0.000    0.000    0.000 {max}
```

48	0.000	0.000	0.000	0.000 {method 'append' of 'list' objects}
1	0.000	0.000	0.000	0.000 {method 'disable' of '_lsprof.Profiler' objects}
1	0.000	0.000	0.000	0.000 {method 'get' of 'dict' objects}
1	0.000	0.000	0.000	0.000 {method 'items' of 'dict' objects}
8	0.000	0.000	0.000	0.000 {min}
6	0.000	0.000	0.000	0.000 {ord}

The `Profile(timer=None, timeunit=0.0, subcalls=True, builtins=True)` method returns a class, providing more control to the developer during the profiling process than `run` and `runctx` do.

The `timer` parameter is a custom function that can be used to measure time in a different way than the one provided by default. It must be a function returning a number representing the current time. If the developer needs a custom function, it should be as fast as possible to lower overhead and avoid problems of calibration (please refer to *A note about limitations* section a few pages back).

If the number returned by the timer is an integer, the `timeunit` parameter specifies the multiplier that represents the duration of each unit of time. For example, if the returned value is in milliseconds, then `timeunit` would be `.001`.

Let's also take a look at the methods provided by the returned class:

- `enable()`: This starts collecting profiling data
- `disable()`: This stops collecting profiling data
- `create_stats()`: This stops collecting data and records the information gathered as the current profile
- `print_stats(sort=-1)`: This creates a `stats` object and prints the result into STDOUT
- `dump_stats(filename)`: This writes the content of the current profile into a file
- `run(cmd)`: This is same as the `run` function we saw earlier
- `runctx(cmd, globals, locals)`: This is same as the `runctx` function we saw earlier
- `runcall(func, *args, **kwargs)`: This gathers profiling information about the function called

Let's see the preceding example, using the following method this time:

```
import cProfile

def runRe():
    import re
    re.compile("foo|bar")

prof = cProfile.Profile()
prof.enable()
runRe()
prof.create_stats()
prof.print_stats()
```

There are more lines involved to get the profiling going, but it is clearly less invasive to the original code. That is an advantage when trying to profile code that's already been written and tested. This way, we can add and remove our profiling code without having to modify the original code.

There is an even less invasive alternative, which involves not adding code at all, but using some specific command-line parameters when running the script instead:

```
$ python -m cProfile your_script.py -o your_script.profile
```

Note that this will profile the entire code, so if you were actually just profiling a specific portion of your script, the preceding approach would not return the same results.

Now, before going into more detailed and interesting examples, let's first look at the Stats class and understand what it can do for us.

The Stats class

The pstats module provides the developer with the Stats class, which, in turn, allows them to read and manipulate the content of the stats file (the file into which we saved the profiling information using one of the methods described earlier).

For example, the following code loads the stats file and prints out the sorted statistics:

```
import pstats
p = pstats.Stats('stats')
p.strip_dirs().sort_stats(-1).print_stats()
```

Note that the Stats class constructor is able to receive a cProfile.Profile instance instead of the file name as the source of the data.

Let's take a closer look at the methods provided by the pstats.Stats class:

- strip_dirs(): This removes all the leading paths' information from the file names in the report. This method modifies the stats instance, so any instance that has this method executed will be considered to have its items in a random order. If two entries are considered to be the same (same line on the same file name having the same function name), then those entries would be accumulated.

- add(*filenames): This method loads more information into stats from the files referenced in the file names. It's worth mentioning that just like with only one file, the stats entries that reference the same function (file name, and line and function name) will be accumulated.

- dump_stats(filename): Just like in the cProfile.Profile class, this method saves the data loaded into the Stats class inside a file.

- sort_stats(*keys): This method is present since version 2.3, and it modifies the stats object by sorting its entries by the given criteria. When more than one criteria is given, then the additional ones are used only when there is equality in the previous ones. For instance, if sort_stats ('name', 'file') is used, it would sort all entries by function name, and when that name is the same, it would sort those entries by file name.

The method is smart enough to understand abbreviations as long as they're unambiguous, so be careful there. The full list of the currently supported sorting criteria is as follows:

Criteria	Meaning	Ascending/Descending
calls	Total number of calls	Descending
cumulative	Cumulative time	Descending
cumtime	Cumulative time	Descending
file	File name	Ascending
filename	File name	Ascending
module	File name	Ascending
ncalls	Total number of calls	Descending
pcalls	Primitive call count	Descending
line	Line number	Ascending

Criteria	Meaning	Ascending/Descending
name	Function name	Ascending
nfl	Composite of name/file/line	Descending
stdname	Standard name	Ascending
time	Internal time	Descending
tottime	Internal time	Descending

A note on nfl versus stdname

The main difference between these two sort types is that the latter is a sort of the printed name. This means the line numbers will be sorted as strings (which means that for 4, 20, and 30 the sorting will be 20, 30, 4). The nfl sort does a numeric comparison of the line number fields.

Finally, for backward compatibility reasons, some numeric values are accepted, instead of the ones in the preceding table. They are -1, 0, 1, and 2, and they're translated into stdname, calls, time, and cumulative, respectively.

- reverse_order(): This method reverses the default order of the sort key selected (so, if the key is by the default ascending order, it would be in the descending order now).

- print_stats(*restrictions): This method takes care of printing out the stats into STDOUT. The optional argument is meant to restrict the output of this function. It can either be an integer value, a decimal value, or a string. They are explained here:
    - integer: This will limit the number of lines printed
    - Decimal between 0.0 and 1.0 (inclusive): This will select the percentage of the lines
    - string: This is a regular expression to match against the standard name

```
        196 function calls (191 primitive calls) in 0.000 seconds

 Random listing order was used
 List reduced from 34 to 10 due to restriction <10>          Reestrictions applied here
 List reduced from 10 to 6 due to restriction <'.*.py.*'>

 ncalls  tottime  percall  cumtime  percall filename:lineno(function)
      1    0.000    0.000    0.000    0.000 /home/fernando/miniconda/lib/python2.7/sre_compile.py:567(compile)
      1    0.000    0.000    0.000    0.000 /home/fernando/miniconda/lib/python2.7/sre_compile.py:256(_optimize_charset)
    3/1    0.000    0.000    0.000    0.000 /home/fernando/miniconda/lib/python2.7/sre_parse.py:151(getwidth)
      1    0.000    0.000    0.000    0.000 /home/fernando/miniconda/lib/python2.7/sre_compile.py:552(_code)
      1    0.000    0.000    0.000    0.000 /home/fernando/miniconda/lib/python2.7/sre_compile.py:228(_compile_charset)
      2    0.000    0.000    0.000    0.000 /home/fernando/miniconda/lib/python2.7/sre_parse.py:206(match)
```

The preceding screenshot shows the output we get from calling the `print_stats` method as follows:

```
import cProfile
import pstats

def runRe():
    import re
    re.compile("foo|bar")
prof = cProfile.Profile()
prof.enable()
runRe()
prof.create_stats()

p = pstats.Stats(prof)
p.print_stats(10, 1.0, '.*.py.*') #print top 10 lines that match the
given reg exp.
```

If more than one parameter is passed, then they are applied sequentially. As we've seen in the preceding lines of code, the output of this profiler can be quite long. However, if we sort it properly, then we can summarize that output using this parameter and still get relevant information.

The `print_callers(*restrictions)` function works with the same input and restriction rules than the previous one, but the output is a bit different. For every function called during the execution of our program, it'll show the number of times each call was made, the total and cumulative times, and a combination of filename, and the line and function names.

Let's look at a quick example of how using `cProfile.Profile` and `Stats` can render the list of caller functions:

```
import cProfile
import pstats

def runRe():
    import re
    re.compile("foo|bar")
prof = cProfile.Profile()
prof.enable()
runRe()
prof.create_stats()

p = pstats.Stats(prof)
p.print_callers()
```

Notice how we're combining the `pstats.Stats` class with the `cProfile.Profile` class. They're working together to gather and show the information in the way we need it. Now, look at the output:

The `print_callees(*restrictions)` method prints a list of functions that call other functions. The format of the data shown and the restrictions are same as the preceding example.

You may encounter a block like the one shown in the following screenshot as part of the output:

This output means that the functions on the right-hand side were called by the same function on the left-hand side.

Profiling examples

Now that we've seen the basics of how to use `cProfile` and `Stats`, let's dig into some more interesting and practical examples.

Fibonacci again

Let's go back to the Fibonacci example, since a basic recursive Fibonacci sequence calculator has a lot of room for improvement.

Let's first look at the unprofiled, unoptimized code:

```
import profile

def fib(n):
    if n <= 1:
  return n
      else:
          return fib(n-1) + fib(n-2)

def fib_seq(n):
    seq = [ ]
    if n > 0:
        seq.extend(fib_seq(n-1))
    seq.append(fib(n))
    return seq

profile.run('print fib_seq(20); print')
```

This code will output the following results:

```
[0, 1, 1, 2, 3, 5, 8, 13, 21, 34, 55, 89, 144, 233, 377, 610, 987, 1597, 2584, 4181, 6765]
         57356 function calls (66 primitive calls) in 0.142 seconds

   Ordered by: standard name

   ncalls  tottime  percall  cumtime  percall filename:lineno(function)
       21    0.001    0.000    0.001    0.000 :0(append)
       20    0.000    0.000    0.000    0.000 :0(extend)
        1    0.000    0.000    0.000    0.000 :0(setprofile)
        1    0.000    0.000    0.142    0.142 <string>:1(<module>)
 57291/21    0.141    0.000    0.141    0.007 B02088_02_08.py:3(fib)
     21/1    0.000    0.000    0.142    0.142 B02088_02_08.py:9(fib_seq)
        1    0.000    0.000    0.142    0.142 profile:0(print fib_seq(20); print)
        0    0.000             0.000          profile:0(profiler)
```

The output is printed correctly, but look at the highlighted sections in the preceding screenshot. These sections are explained here:

- There are 57.356 function calls during those 0.114 seconds
- Out of those, only 66 were primitive calls (not called by recursion)
- In line 3 of our code, 57.270 (57.291 − 21) were recursion-induced function calls

As we all know, the act of calling another function adds an overhead to our time. Since it looks like (for the cumtime column) that most of the execution time is spent inside this function, we can safely assume that if we speed this up, the entire script's time would be affected.

Now, let's apply a simple decorator to the fib function that will allow us to cache the previously calculated values (a technique also known as memoization, about which you'll read in the upcoming chapters) so that we don't have to call fib more than once per value:

```python
import profile

class cached:
    def __init__(self, fn):
        self.fn = fn
        self.cache = {}

    def __call__(self, *args):
        try:
            return self.cache[args]
        except KeyError:
            self.cache[args] = self.fn(*args)
            return self.cache[args]

@cached
def fib(n):
    if n <= 1:
        return n
    else:
        return fib(n-1) + fib(n-2)

def fib_seq(n):
    seq = [ ]
    if n > 0:

        seq.extend(fib_seq(n-1))
    seq.append(fib(n))
    return seq

profile.run('print fib_seq(20); print')
```

Now, let's run the code again and look at the output:

```
[0, 1, 1, 2, 3, 5, 8, 13, 21, 34, 55, 89, 144, 233, 377, 610, 987, 1597, 2584, 4181, 6765]

         145 function calls (87 primitive calls) in 0.001 seconds

   Ordered by: standard name

   ncalls  tottime  percall  cumtime  percall filename:lineno(function)
       21    0.000    0.000    0.000    0.000 :0(append)
       20    0.000    0.000    0.000    0.000 :0(extend)
        1    0.000    0.000    0.000    0.000 :0(setprofile)
        1    0.000    0.000    0.001    0.001 <string>:1(<module>)
       21    0.000    0.000    0.000    0.000 B02088_02_09.py:15(fib)
     21/1    0.000    0.000    0.001    0.001 B02088_02_09.py:22(fib_seq)
    59/21    0.000    0.000    0.000    0.000 B02088_02_09.py:8(__call__)
        1    0.000    0.000    0.001    0.001 profile:0(print fib_seq(20); print)
        0    0.000             0.000          profile:0(profiler)
```

We went from around 57k total calls to only 145 and from 0.114 seconds to 0.001.
That's an amazing improvement! However, we have more primitive calls, but we
also have significantly less recursive calls.

Let's continue with another possible optimization. Our example works quite fast for
a single call, but let's try to do several runs in a row and get the combined stats for
that execution. Perhaps, we'll get something interesting back. To do this, we need to
use the stats module. Let's see an example for this:

```
import cProfile
import pstats
from fibo4 import fib, fib_seq

filenames = []
profiler = cProfile.Profile()
profiler.enable()
for i in range(5):
    print fib_seq(1000); print
profiler.create_stats()
stats = pstats.Stats(profiler)
stats.strip_dirs().sort_stats('cumulative').print_stats()
stats.print_callers()
```

We've pushed the envelope here. Getting the Fibonacci sequence for 1000 might be too much to ask, especially from a recursive implementation. Indeed, we ran out of recursion depth. This is mainly due to the fact that cPython has a guard to prevent a stack overflow error generated by the amount of recursive calls (ideally, a tail recursion optimization would solve this, but cPython does not provide it). So, we just found another issue. Let's try to fix it and reanalyze the code:

```
import profile
def fib(n):
    a, b = 0, 1
    for i in range(0, n):
        a,b = b, a+b
    return a

def fib_seq(n):
    seq = [ ]
    for i in range(0, n + 1):
        seq.append(fib(i))
    return seq

print fib_seq(1000)
```

The preceding lines of code print a huge list of really big numbers, but these lines prove that we made it. We can now compute the Fibonacci sequence for the number 1000. Now, let's analyze it and see what we find.

Using the new profiling code, but requiring the iterative version of the Fibonacci implementation, we will get this:

```
import cProfile
import pstats
from fibo_iter import fib, fib_seq

filenames = []
profiler = cProfile.Profile()
profiler.enable()
for i in range(5):
    print fib_seq(1000); print
profiler.create_stats()
stats = pstats.Stats(profiler)
stats.strip_dirs().sort_stats('cumulative').print_stats()
stats.print_callers()
```

This, in turn, will yield the following result into the console:

```
        15028 function calls in 0.187 seconds

  Ordered by: cumulative time

  ncalls  tottime  percall  cumtime  percall filename:lineno(function)
       5    0.002    0.000    0.187    0.037 fibo_iter.py:10(fib_seq)
    5005    0.173    0.000    0.184    0.000 fibo_iter.py:3(fib)
    5011    0.011    0.000    0.011    0.000 {range}
    5005    0.001    0.000    0.001    0.000 {method 'append' of 'list' objects}
       1    0.000    0.000    0.000    0.000 cProfile.py:90(create_stats)
       1    0.000    0.000    0.000    0.000 {method 'disable' of '_lsprof.Profiler' objects}


  Ordered by: cumulative time

Function                                          was called by...
                                                    ncalls  tottime  cumtime
fibo_iter.py:10(fib_seq)                          <-
fibo_iter.py:3(fib)                               <-    5005    0.173    0.184  fibo_iter.py:10(fib_seq)
{range}                                           <-    5005    0.011    0.011  fibo_iter.py:3(fib)
                                                          5    0.000    0.000  fibo_iter.py:10(fib_seq)
{method 'append' of 'list' objects}               <-    5005    0.001    0.001  fibo_iter.py:10(fib_seq)
cProfile.py:90(create_stats)                      <-
{method 'disable' of '_lsprof.Profiler' objects}  <-       1    0.000    0.000  cProfile.py:90(create_stats)
```

Our new code is taking 0.187 seconds to calculate the Fibonacci sequence of 1000 five times. It's not a bad number, but we know we can improve it by caching the results, just like we did earlier. *As you can see, we have 5005 calls to the* `fib` *function. If we cache it, we would have a lot less function calls, which would mean less execution time.*

With very little effort, we can improve that time by caching the calls to the `fib` function, which, according the preceding report, is called 5005 times:

```python
import profile

class cached:
    def __init__(self, fn):
        self.fn = fn
        self.cache = {}

    def __call__(self, *args):
        try:
            return self.cache[args]
        except KeyError:
            self.cache[args] = self.fn(*args)
            return self.cache[args]

@cached
def fib(n):
    a, b = 0, 1
    for i in range(0, n):
```

```
        a,b = b, a+b
    return a


def fib_seq(n):
    seq = [ ]
    for i in range(0, n + 1):
        seq.append(fib(i))
    return seq


print fib_seq(1000)
```

You should get something like the following output:

```
  10023 function calls in 0.006 seconds

Ordered by: cumulative time

ncalls  tottime  percall  cumtime  percall filename:lineno(function)
     5    0.004    0.001    0.006    0.001 fibo_iter.py:25(fib_seq)
  5005    0.002    0.000    0.002    0.000 fibo_iter.py:8(__call__)
  5005    0.000    0.000    0.000    0.000 {method 'append' of 'list' objects}
     6    0.000    0.000    0.000    0.000 {range}
     1    0.000    0.000    0.000    0.000 cProfile.py:90(create_stats)
     1    0.000    0.000    0.000    0.000 {method 'disable' of '_lsprof.Profiler' objects}


Ordered by: cumulative time

Function                                         was called by...
                                                    ncalls  tottime  cumtime
fibo_iter.py:25(fib_seq)                         <-
fibo_iter.py:8(__call__)                         <-   5005    0.002    0.002  fibo_iter.py:25(fib_seq)
{method 'append' of 'list' objects}              <-   5005    0.000    0.000  fibo_iter.py:25(fib_seq)
{range}                                          <-      5    0.000    0.000  fibo_iter.py:25(fib_seq)
cProfile.py:90(create_stats)                     <-
{method 'disable' of '_lsprof.Profiler' objects} <-      1    0.000    0.000  cProfile.py:90(create_stats)
```

Simply by caching the call to `fib`, we went from 0.187 seconds to 0.006 seconds. This is an amazing improvement. Well done!

Tweet stats

Let's look at another example, something a bit more conceptually complex, since calculating the Fibonacci sequence is not really an everyday use case. Let's do something a bit more interesting. These days, Twitter allows you to download your complete list of tweets in the form of a CSV file. We'll use this file to generate some statistics from our feed.

Using the data provided, we'll calculate the following statistics:

- The percentage of messages that are actual replies
- The percentage of tweets that were made from the website (https://twitter.com)
- The percentage of tweets that were made from a mobile phone

The output form our script will look like the one shown in the following screenshot:

```
-------- My twitter stats -------------
35% of tweets are replies
86% of tweets were made from the website
13% of tweets were made from my phone
```

To keep things simple, we'll take care of parsing the CSV file and doing these basic calculations. We won't use any third-party modules; that way, we'll be in total control of the code and its analysis. This means leaving out obvious things, such as using the CSV module from Python.

Other bad practices shown earlier, such as the inc_stat function or the fact that we're loading the entire file into memory before processing it, will remind you that this is just an example to show basic improvements.

Here is the initial code of the script:

```python
def build_twit_stats():
    STATS_FILE = './files/tweets.csv'
    STATE = {
        'replies': 0,
        'from_web': 0,
        'from_phone': 0,
        'lines_parts': [],
        'total_tweets': 0
    }
    read_data(STATE, STATS_FILE)
    get_stats(STATE)
    print_results(STATE)

def get_percentage(n, total):
    return (n * 100) / total

def read_data(state, source):
```

```
        f = open(source, 'r')

        lines = f.read().strip().split("\"\n\"")
        for line in lines:

            state['lines_parts'].append(line.strip().split(','))
        state['total_tweets'] = len(lines)

    def inc_stat(state, st):
        state[st] += 1

    def get_stats(state):
        for i in state['lines_parts']:
            if(i[1] != '""'):
                inc_stat(state, 'replies')
            if(i[4].find('Twitter Web Client') > -1):
                inc_stat(state, 'from_web')
            else:
                inc_stat(state, 'from_phone')

    def print_results(state):
        print "-------- My twitter stats ------------"
        print "%s%% of tweets are replies" %
        (get_percentage(state['replies'], state['total_tweets']))
        print "%s%% of tweets were made from the website" %
        (get_percentage(state['from_web'], state['total_tweets']))
        print "%s%% of tweets were made from my phone" %
        (get_percentage(state['from_phone'], state['total_tweets']))
```

To be fair, the code doesn't do anything too complicated. It loads the content of the file, splits it into lines, and then it splits each line into different fields. Finally, it counts things. One might think that with this explanation, there is nothing much to optimize, but we're about to see that there is always room for some optimization.

Another important thing to note is that the CSV file we'll be processing has almost 150 MB of tweets data.

Here is the script that imports that code, uses it, and generates a profiling report:

```
import cProfile
import pstats

from B02088_02_14 import build_twit_stats
```

```
profiler = cProfile.Profile()

profiler.enable()

build_twit_stats()

profiler.create_stats()
stats = pstats.Stats(profiler)
stats.strip_dirs().sort_stats('cumulative').print_stats()
```

The output we get from this execution is as follows:

```
--------- My twitter stats -------------
34% of tweets are replies
86% of tweets were made from the website
13% of tweets were made from my phone                 1
       3019962 function calls in 2.059 seconds

   Ordered by: cumulative time

3  ncalls  tottime  percall  cumtime  2  percall filename:lineno(function)
        1    0.026    0.026    2.059     2.059 B02988_02_14.py:6(build_twit_stats)
        1    0.262    0.262    1.582     1.582 B02988_02_14.py:22(read_data)
   564851    1.031    0.000    1.031     0.000 {method 'split' of 'str' objects}
        1    0.257    0.257    0.450     0.450 B02988_02_14.py:33(get_stats)
   564851    0.226    0.000    0.226     0.000 {method 'strip' of 'str' objects}
   760548    0.099    0.000    0.099     0.000 B02988_02_14.py:30(inc_stat)
   564850    0.095    0.000    0.095     0.000 {method 'find' of 'str' objects}
        1    0.039    0.039    0.039     0.039 {method 'read' of 'file' objects}
   564850    0.024    0.000    0.024     0.000 {method 'append' of 'list' objects}
        1    0.000    0.000    0.000     0.000 B02988_02_14.py:42(print_results)
        1    0.000    0.000    0.000     0.000 {open}
        1    0.000    0.000    0.000     0.000 cProfile.py:90(create_stats)
        1    0.000    0.000    0.000     0.000 {len}
        3    0.000    0.000    0.000     0.000 B02988_02_14.py:19(get_percentage)
        1    0.000    0.000    0.000     0.000 {method 'disable' of '_lsprof.Profiler' objects}
```

There are three main areas of interest in the preceding screenshot:

1. Total execution time
2. Cumulative times of individual function calls
3. Total number of calls for individual functions

Our aim is to lower the total execution time. For that, we will pay special attention to the cumulative times of individual functions and the total number of calls for individual functions. We can infer the following conclusions for the last two points:

- The `build_twit_stats` function is the one that takes the most time. However, as you can see in the preceding lines of code, it just calls all other functions, so it makes sense. We can focus on `read_data` since it's the second most time-consuming function. This is interesting, because it means that our bottleneck is not when we calculate the stats, but when we load the data for it.

- In the third line of the code, we also see exactly our bottleneck inside `read_data`. We perform too many `split` commands and they add up.

- We also see that the fourth most time-consuming function is `get_stats`.

So, let's tackle these issues and see if we get better results. The biggest bottleneck we had was the way we were loading data. We were loading it all into memory first and then iterating over it to calculate our stats. We can improve this by reading the file line by line and calculating the stats after each one. Let's see how that code would look.

The new `read_data` method looks like this:

```
def read_data(state, source):
  f = open(source)

  buffer_parts = []
  for line in f:
    #Multi line tweets are saved in several lines in the file,
    so we need to
    #take that into account.
    parts = line.split('","')
    buffer_parts += parts
    if len(parts) == 10:
      state['lines_parts'].append(buffer_parts)
      get_line_stats(state, buffer_parts)
      buffer_parts = []
  state['total_tweets'] = len(state['lines_parts'])
```

We had to add some logic to take into account multiline tweets, which are also saved as multiline records on our CSV file. We changed our `get_stats` function into `get_line_stats`, which simplifies its logic since it only calculates the values for the current record:

```
def get_line_stats(state, line_parts):
  if line_parts[1] != '' :
    state['replies'] += 1
```

```
if 'Twitter Web Client' in line_parts[4]:
    state['from_web'] += 1
else:
    state['from_phone'] += 1
```

The two final improvements were to remove the calls to inc_stat, since, thanks to the dictionary we're using, the call is unnecessary. We also replaced the usage of the find method using the more proficient in operator.

Let's run the code again and see the changes:

```
-------- My twitter stats --------------
34% of tweets are replies
86% of tweets were made from the website
13% of tweets were made from my phone
        2312158 function calls in 1.590 seconds

  Ordered by: cumulative time

  ncalls  tottime  percall  cumtime  percall filename:lineno(function)
       1    0.000    0.000    1.590    1.590 B02088_02_16.py:3(build_twit_stats)
       1    0.607    0.607    1.589    1.589 B02088_02_16.py:19(read_data)
  604612    0.750    0.000    0.750    0.000 {method 'split' of 'str' objects}
  551462    0.173    0.000    0.173    0.000 B02088_02_16.py:38(get_line_stats)
  604613    0.033    0.000    0.033    0.000 {len}
  551462    0.027    0.000    0.027    0.000 {method 'append' of 'list' objects}
       1    0.000    0.000    0.000    0.000 B02088_02_16.py:46(print_results)
       3    0.000    0.000    0.000    0.000 B02088_02_16.py:16(get_percentage)
       1    0.000    0.000    0.000    0.000 {open}
       1    0.000    0.000    0.000    0.000 cProfile.py:90(create_stats)
       1    0.000    0.000    0.000    0.000 {method 'disable' of '_lsprof.Profiler' objects}
```

We went from 2 seconds to 1.6; that was a considerable improvement. The read_data function is still up there with the most time-consuming functions, but that's just because it now also calls the get_line_stats function. We can also improve on this, since even though the get_line_stats function does very little, we're incurring in a lookup time by calling it so often inside the loop. We could inline this function and see if that helps.

The new code would look like this:

```
def read_data(state, source):
    f = open(source)

    buffer_parts = []
    for line in f:
        #Multi line tweets are saved in several lines in the file,
        so we need to
        #take that into account.
```

```
        parts = line.split('","')
        buffer_parts += parts
        if len(parts) == 10:
          state['lines_parts'].append(buffer_parts)
          if buffer_parts[1] != '' :
            state['replies'] += 1
          if 'Twitter Web Client' in buffer_parts[4]:
            state['from_web'] += 1
          else:
            state['from_phone'] += 1
          buffer_parts = []
    state['total_tweets'] = len(state['lines_parts'])
```

Now, with the new changes, the report will look like this:

```
-------- My twitter stats -------------
34% of tweets are replies
86% of tweets were made from the website
13% of tweets were made from my phone
        1760696 function calls in 1.423 seconds

  Ordered by: cumulative time

  ncalls  tottime  percall  cumtime  percall filename:lineno(function)
       1    0.000    0.000    1.423    1.423 B02088_02_16.py:3(build_twit_stats)
       1    0.624    0.624    1.423    1.423 B02088_02_16.py:19(read_data)
  604612    0.746    0.000    0.746    0.000 {method 'split' of 'str' objects}
  604613    0.028    0.000    0.028    0.000 {len}
  551462    0.025    0.000    0.025    0.000 {method 'append' of 'list' objects}
       1    0.000    0.000    0.000    0.000 B02088_02_16.py:40(print_results)
       1    0.000    0.000    0.000    0.000 cProfile.py:90(create_stats)
       1    0.000    0.000    0.000    0.000 {open}
       3    0.000    0.000    0.000    0.000 B02088_02_16.py:16(get_percentage)
       1    0.000    0.000    0.000    0.000 {method 'disable' of '_lsprof.Profiler' objects}
```

There is a notable improvement between the first screenshot and the preceding one. We got the time down to barely above 1.4 seconds from 2 seconds. The number of function calls is considerably lower as well (it went from around 3 million calls to 1.7 million), which in turn should help lower the time spent doing lookups and calls.

As an added bonus, we will improve the readability of our code by simplifying it. Here is the final code all together:

```
def build_twit_stats():
    STATS_FILE = './files/tweets.csv'
    STATE = {
        'replies': 0,
        'from_web': 0,
```

```
        'from_phone': 0,
        'lines_parts': [],
        'total_tweets': 0
    }
    read_data(STATE, STATS_FILE)
    print_results(STATE)

def get_percentage(n, total):
    return (n * 100) / total

def read_data(state, source):
    f = open(source)

    buffer_parts = []
    for line in f:
        #Multi line tweets are saved in several lines in the file,
        so we need to
        #take that into account.
        parts = line.split('","')
        buffer_parts += parts
        if len(parts) == 10:
            state['lines_parts'].append(buffer_parts)
            if buffer_parts[1] != '' :
                state['replies'] += 1
            if 'Twitter Web Client' in buffer_parts[4]:
                state['from_web'] += 1
            else:
                state['from_phone'] += 1
            buffer_parts = []
    state['total_tweets'] = len(state['lines_parts'])

def print_results(state):
    print "-------- My twitter stats -------------"

    print "%s%% of tweets are replies" %
    (get_percentage(state['replies'], state['total_tweets']))

    print "%s%% of tweets were made from the website" %
    (get_percentage(state['from_web'], state['total_tweets']))

    print "%s%% of tweets were made from my phone" %
    (get_percentage(state['from_phone'], state['total_tweets']))
```

This is it for our review of cProfile. With it, we managed to profile our scripts, getting per-function numbers and total function calls. It helped us improve on the overall view of the system. We'll now look at a different profiler, which will give us per-line details that cProfile is not capable of providing.

line_profiler

This profiler is different from cProfile. It helps you profile a function line by line instead of doing a deterministic profiling, like the other one does.

To install this profiler, you can use the pip (https://pypi.python.org/pypi/pip) command-line tool, with the following command:

```
$ pip install line_profiler
```

> If you run into any trouble, such as missing files during installation, make sure you have all development dependencies installed. In the case of Ubuntu, you can ensure that all the dependencies are installed by running the following command:
>
> ```
> $ sudo apt-get install python-dev libxml2-dev
> libxslt-dev
> ```

This profiler is trying to fill in a breach left by cProfile and others like it. Other profilers cover CPU time on function calls. Most of the time, this is more than enough to catch the problems and fix them (we saw that earlier). However, sometimes, the problem or bottleneck is related to one specific line inside the function and that is where line_profiler comes into play.

The author recommends us to use the kernprof utility, so we'll look at examples of it. Kernprof will create an instance of the profiler and insert it into the __builtins__ namespace with the name, profile. The profiler was designed to be used as a decorator, so you can just decorate any function you want, and it will time the execution for each line of it.

This is how we'll execute the profiler:

```
$ kernprof -l script_to_profile.py
```

The decorated function is ready to be profiled:

```
@profile
def fib(n):
    a, b = 0, 1
    for i in range(0, n):
        a,b = b, a+b
    return a
```

By default, `kernprof` will save the results into a file called `script_to_profile.py.lprof`, but you can tell it to display the results right away using the `-v` attribute:

$ kernprof -l -v script_to_profile.py

Here is a simple example output to help you understand what you'll be looking at:

```
Wrote profile results to kernprof-test.py.lprof
Timer unit: 1e-06 s

Total time: 7.3e-05 s
File: kernprof-test.py
Function: test at line 2

Line #      Hits         Time  Per Hit   % Time  Line Contents
==============================================================
     2                                           @profile
     3                                           def test():
     4        11            5      0.5      6.8       for i in range(0, 10):
     5        10           63      6.3     36.3           print i**2
     6         1            5      5.0      6.8       print "End of the function"
```

The output contains every line of the function, next to the timing information. There are six columns of information, and this is what they mean:

- `Line #`: This is the line number inside the file.
- `Hits`: This is the number of times this line is executed during the profiling.
- `Time`: This is the total execution time of that line, specified in timer's unit. In the header information before the table with the results, you'll notice a field called `Timer unit`, that number is the conversion factor to seconds (to calculate the actual time, you'll have to do time x timer's unit). It might be different on different systems.
- `Per hit`: The average amount of time spent executing that line of code. This is also specified in timer's units.
- `% Time`: The percentage of time spent executing that line, relative to the total time spent executing the entire function.

If you're building another tool that leverages line_profiler, there are two ways to let it know which functions to profile: using the constructor and using the add_function method.

The line_profiler also provides the same run, runctx, runcall, enable, and disable methods that cProfile.Profile provides. However, the last two aren't safe when nesting, so be careful. After profiling, you can dump the stats into a file using the dump_stats(filename) method, or you can print them using the print_stats([stream]) method. It'll print the results into sys.stdout or whatever other stream you pass it as parameter.

Here is an example of the same function from earlier. This time, the function is being profiled using the line_profiler API:

```
import line_profiler
import sys

def test():
    for i in range(0, 10):
        print i**2
    print "End of the function"


prof = line_profiler.LineProfiler(test) #pass in the function to
profile

prof.enable() #start profiling
test()
prof.disable() #stop profiling

prof.print_stats(sys.stdout) #print out the results
```

kernprof

The kernprof is the profiling utility that comes bundled with line_profiler and allows us to abstract most of the profiling code from our own source code. This means we can use it to profile our application, like we saw earlier. kernprof will do several things for us:

- It'll work with cProfile, lsprof, and even the profile module, depending on which one is available.
- It'll find our script properly. If the script is not inside the current folder, it'll even check the PATH variable.

- It'll instantiate and insert the profiler into the `__builtins__` namespace with the name `profile`. This will allow us to use the profiler inside our code. In the case of `line_profiler`, we can even use it as a decorator without having to worry about importing anything.

- The output files with the profiling `stats` can be viewed using the `pstats.Stats` class or even from the command line as follows:

```
$ python -m pstats stats_file.py.prof
```

Or in the case of `lprof` files:

```
$ python -m line_profiler stats_file.py.lprof
```

Some things to consider about kernprof

There are a couple of things to take into consideration when reading the output from kernprof. In some cases, the output might be confusing, or the numbers might not add up. Here are the answers to some of the most common questions:

- **Line-by-line time doesn't add up to total time when the profile function calls another one**: When profiling a function that gets called by another profiled function, sometimes, it might happen that the numbers don't add up. This is because `kernprof` is only recording the time spent inside the function and tries to avoid measuring any overhead added by the profiler itself, as shown in the following screenshot:

```
Timer unit: 1e-06 s

Total time: 0.010539 s
File: kernprof-test3.py
Function: printI at line 3

Line #      Hits         Time  Per Hit   % Time  Line Contents
==============================================================
     3                                           @profile
     4                                           def printI(i):
     5         10            3      0.3      0.0      counter = 0
     6      20010         5029      0.3     47.7      for a in range(0, 2000):
     7      20000         5427      0.3     51.5          counter +=1
     8         10           80      8.0      0.8      print i ** 2

Total time: 0.019611 s
File: kernprof-test3.py
Function: test at line 10

Line #      Hits         Time  Per Hit   % Time  Line Contents
==============================================================
    10                                           @profile
    11                                           def test():
    12         11           39      3.5      0.2      for i in range(0, 10):
    13         10        19567   1956.7     99.8          printI(i)
    14          1            5      5.0      0.0      print "End of the function"
```

The preceding screenshot shows an example of this. The `printI` function takes `0.010539` seconds according to the profiler. However, inside the `test` function, the total amount of time spent seems to be `19567` timer's units, which amounts to `0.019567` seconds.

- **List comprehension lines have a lot more hits than they should inside the report**: This is basically because the report is adding one hit per iteration inside the expression. Here is an example of this:

```
Timer unit: 1e-06 s

Total time: 6.7e-05 s
File: kernprof-test3.py
Function: printExpression at line 2

Line #      Hits         Time  Per Hit   % Time  Line Contents
==============================================================
     2                                           @profile
     3                                           def printExpression():
     4       102           27      0.3     40.3       myList = [x for x in xrange(0, 50)]
     5         2           40     20.0     59.7       print myList

Total time: 0.00011 s
File: kernprof-test3.py
Function: test at line 7

Line #      Hits         Time  Per Hit   % Time  Line Contents
==============================================================
     7                                           @profile
     8                                           def test():
     9         1           69     69.0     62.7       printExpression()
    10         1           37     37.0     33.6       printExpression()
    11         1            4      4.0      3.6       print "End of the function"
```

You can see how the actual expression line has `102` hits, `2` for each time the `printExpression` function is called, and the other 100 due to the range used.

Profiling examples

Now that we've seen the basics of how to use `line_profiler` and `kernprof`, let's get our hands dirty with more interesting examples.

Back to Fibonacci

Yes, let's again profile our original Fibonacci code. It'll be good to compare the output from both profilers to see how they work.

```
[0, 1, 1, 2, 3, 5, 8, 13, 21, 34, 55, 89, 144, 233, 377, 610, 987, 1597, 2584, 4181, 6765]
Wrote profile results to basic-fibo.py.lprof
Timer unit: 1e-06 s

Total time: 0.039405 s
File: basic-fibo.py
Function: fib at line 2

Line #      Hits         Time  Per Hit   % Time  Line Contents
==============================================================
     2                                           @profile
     3                                           def fib(n):
     4     57291        12857      0.2     32.6       if n <= 1:
     5     28656         5604      0.2     14.2           return n
     6                                               else:
     7     28635        20944      0.7     53.2           return fib(n-1) + fib(n-2)

Total time: 0.111788 s
File: basic-fibo.py
Function: fib_seq at line 9

Line #      Hits         Time  Per Hit   % Time  Line Contents
==============================================================
     9                                           @profile
    10                                           def fib_seq(n):
    11        21            7      0.3      0.0       seq = [ ]
    12        21            6      0.3      0.0       if n > 0:
    13        20           79      4.0      0.1           seq.extend(fib_seq(n-1))
    14        21       111690   5318.6     99.9       seq.append(fib(n))
    15        21            6      0.3      0.0       return seq
```

Out of all the numbers in the report, we can rest assured that timing is not an issue. Inside the `fib` function, none of the lines take too long (nor should they). Inside `fib_seq`, only one does, but that's because of the recursion shown inside `fib`.

So, our problem (as we already know) is the recursion and the number of times we're executing the `fib` function (57, 291 times to be exact). Every time we make a function call, the interpreter has to do a lookup by name and then execute the function. Every time we call the `fib` function, two more calls are made.

The first thing that comes to mind is to somehow lower the number of recursive calls. We can rewrite it into an iterative version or do a quick fix by adding the cached decorator, like we did earlier. We can see the results in the following report:

```
[0, 1, 1, 2, 3, 5, 8, 13, 21, 34, 55, 89, 144, 233, 377, 610, 987, 1597, 2584, 4181, 6765]
Wrote profile results to basic-fibo.py.lprof
Timer unit: 1e-06 s

Total time: 4.7e-05 s
File: basic-fibo.py
Function: fib at line 15

Line #      Hits         Time  Per Hit   % Time  Line Contents
==============================================================
    15                                           @cached
    16                                           @profile
    17                                           def fib(n):
    18         21            7      0.3     14.9      if n <= 1:
    19          2            1      0.5      2.1          return n
    20                                               else:
    21         19           39      2.1     83.0          return fib(n-1) + fib(n-2)

Total time: 0.000225 s
File: basic-fibo.py
Function: fib_seq at line 23

Line #      Hits         Time  Per Hit   % Time  Line Contents
==============================================================
    23                                           @profile
    24                                           def fib_seq(n):
    25         21            2      0.1      0.9      seq = [ ]
    26         21            5      0.2      2.2      if n > 0:
    27         20           64      3.2     28.4          seq.extend(fib_seq(n-1))
    28         21          149      7.1     66.2      seq.append(fib(n))
    29         21            5      0.2      2.2      return seq
```

The number of hits for the `fib` function went from 57, 291 hits to `21`. This is another proof that the cached decorator is a great optimization in this case.

Inverted index

Instead of repeating the second example from within a different profiler, let's look at another problem: creating an inverted index (http://en.wikipedia.org/wiki/inverted_index).

An inverted index is a resource used by many search engines to find words in several files at the same time. The way they work is by pre-scanning all files, splitting their content into words, and then saving the relations between those words and the files (some even save the position of the word too). This way, when a search is made on a specific word, the searching time is `O(1)` (constant).

Let's see a simple example:

```
//With these files:
file1.txt = "This is a file"
file2.txt = "This is another file"
//We get the following index:
This, (file1.txt, 0), (file2.txt, 0)
is, (file1.txt, 5), (file2.txt, 5)
a, (file1.txt, 8)
another, (file2.txt, 8)
file, (file1.txt, 10), (file2.txt, 16)
```

So now, if we were to look for the word `file`, we know it's in both files (at different positions). Let's see the code that calculates this index (again, the point of the following code is to show classic improvement opportunities, so stick with us until we see the optimized version of the code):

```python
#!/usr/bin/env python

import sys
import os
import glob

def getFileNames(folder):
    return glob.glob("%s/*.txt" % folder)

def getOffsetUpToWord(words, index):
    if not index:
        return 0
    subList = words[0:index]
    length = sum(len(w) for w in subList)
    return length + index + 1

def getWords(content, filename, wordIndexDict):
    STRIP_CHARS = ",.\t\n |"
    currentOffset = 0

    for line in content:
        line = line.strip(STRIP_CHARS)
        localWords = line.split()
        for (idx, word) in enumerate(localWords):
            word = word.strip(STRIP_CHARS)
            if word not in wordIndexDict:
```

```python
        wordIndexDict[word] = []

      line_offset = getOffsetUpToWord(localWords, idx)
      index = (line_offset) + currentOffset
      currentOffset = index
      wordIndexDict[word].append([filename, index])

  return wordIndexDict

def readFileContent(filepath):
    f = open(filepath, 'r')
    return f.read().split( ' ' )

def list2dict(list):
  res = {}
  for item in list:
    if item[0] not in res:
      res[item[0]] = []
    res[item[0]].append(item[1])
  return res

def saveIndex(index):
  lines = []
  for word in index:
    indexLine = ""
    glue = ""
    for filename in index[word]:
      indexLine += "%s(%s, %s)" % (glue, filename,
      ','.join(map(str, index[word][filename])))
      glue = ","
    lines.append("%s, %s" % (word, indexLine))

  f = open("index-file.txt", "w")
  f.write("\n".join(lines))
  f.close()

def __start__():
  files = getFileNames('./files')
  words = {}
  for f in files:
    content = readFileContent(f)
    words = getWords(content, f, words)
```

```
for word in (words):
    words[word] = list2dict(words[word])
saveIndex(words)

__start__()
```

The preceding code is as simple as it gets. It gets the job done for simple .txt files, and that is what we want right now. It'll load all .txt files inside the files folder, split their content into words, and calculate the offset of those words inside the document. Finally, it'll save all this information into a file called index-file.txt.

So, let's begin profiling and see what we get. Since we don't really know exactly which are the heavy-duty functions and which ones are the light ones, let's add the @profile decorator to all of them and run the profiler.

getOffsetUpToWord

The getOffsetUpToWord function looks like a great candidate for optimization, since it gets called quite a few times during execution. Let's keep the decorator on it for now.

```
Total time: 1.45378 s
File: mapper.py
Function: getOffsetUpToWord at line 12

Line #      Hits         Time  Per Hit   % Time  Line Contents
==============================================================
    12                                           @profile
    13                                           def getOffsetUpToWord(words, index):
    14    313868        81878      0.3      5.6       if not index:
    15     29682         7582      0.3      0.5           return 0
    16    284186       106398      0.4      7.3       subList = words[0:index]
    17    284186        70307      0.2      4.8       length = 0
    18   1998159       597693      0.3     41.1       for w in subList:
    19   1713973       514410      0.3     35.4           length += len(w)
    20    284186        75512      0.3      5.2       return length + index + 1
```

getWords

The getWords function does a lot of processing. It even has two nested for loops, so we'll keep the decorator on as well.

```
Total time: 4.00185 s
File: mapper.py
Function: getWords at line 23

Line #      Hits         Time  Per Hit   % Time  Line Contents
==============================================================
    23                                           @profile
    24                                           def getWords(content, filename, wordIndexDict):
    25
    26           2            2      1.0      0.0      STRIP_CHARS = ",.\t\n |"
    27           2            1      0.5      0.0      currentOffset = 0
    28
    29
    30       38858        13798      0.4      0.3      for line in content:
    31       38856        18337      0.5      0.5          line = line.strip(STRIP_CHARS)
    32       38856        35749      0.9      0.9          localWords = line.split()
    33      352724       143714      0.4      3.6          for (idx, word) in enumerate(localWords):
    34      313868       139410      0.4      3.5              word = word.strip(STRIP_CHARS)
    35      313868       170350      0.5      4.3              if word not in wordIndexDict:
    36       42527        19517      0.5      0.5                  wordIndexDict[word] = []
    37
    38      313868      3058664      9.7     76.4              line_offset = getOffsetUpToWord(localWords, idx)
    39      313868       113722      0.4      2.8              index = (line_offset) + currentOffset
    40      313868       109872      0.4      2.7              currentOffset = index
    41      313868       178715      0.6      4.5              wordIndexDict[word].append([filename, index])
    42
    43           2            0      0.0      0.0      return wordIndexDict
```

list2dict

The list2dict function takes care of grabbing a list of arrays with two elements and returning a dictionary, using the first element of the array items as key and the second one as values. We'll leave the @profile decorator on for now.

```
Total time: 0.448933 s
File: mapper.py
Function: list2dict at line 50

Line #      Hits         Time  Per Hit   % Time  Line Contents
==============================================================
    50                                           @profile
    51                                           def list2dict(list):
    52       42527        14268      0.3      3.2      res = {}
    53      356395       116712      0.3     26.0      for item in list:
    54      313868       139029      0.4     31.0          if item[0] not in res:
    55       46535        14948      0.3      3.3              res[item[0]] = []
    56      313868       154092      0.5     34.3          res[item[0]].append(item[1])
    57       42527         9884      0.2      2.2      return res
```

readFileContent

The readFileContent function has two lines, and the significant one simply calls the split method on the content of the file. There is not a lot to improve here, so we'll discard it and focus on the other ones.

```
Total time: 0.003255 s
File: mapper.py
Function: readFileContent at line 45

Line #      Hits         Time  Per Hit   % Time  Line Contents
==============================================================
    45                                            @profile
    46                                            def readFileContent(filepath):
    47           2           23     11.5      0.7      f = open(filepath, 'r')
    48           2         3232   1616.0     99.3      return f.read().split( '\n' )
```

saveIndex

The saveIndex function writes the results of the processing to a file, using a specific format. We might be able to get some better numbers here too.

```
Total time: 0.23337 s
File: mapper.py
Function: saveIndex at line 59

Line #      Hits        Time  Per Hit   % Time  Line Contents
==============================================================
    59                                            @profile
    60                                            def saveIndex(index):
    61           1            0      0.0      0.0      lines = []
    62       42528        17454      0.4      7.5      for word in index:
    63       42527        14588      0.3      6.3          indexLine = ""
    64       42527        13140      0.3      5.6          glue = ""
    65       89062        37775      0.4     16.2          for filename in index[word]:
    66       46535       105780      2.3     45.3              indexLine += "%s(%s, %s)" % (glue, filename, ','.join(map(str, index[word][filename])))
    67       46535        15861      0.3      6.8              glue = ","
    68       42527        24191      0.6     10.4          lines.append("%s, %s" % (word, indexLine))
    69
    70           1          423    423.0      0.2      f = open("index-file.txt", "w")
    71           1         3783   3783.0      1.6      f.write("\n".join(lines))
    72           1          375    375.0      0.2      f.close()
```

__start__

Finally, the main method, __start__, takes care of calling the other functions and doesn't do much heavy lifting, so we'll also discard it.

```
Total time: 6.09869 s
File: mapper.py
Function: __start__ at line 74

Line #      Hits         Time  Per Hit   % Time  Line Contents
==============================================================
    74                                           @profile
    75                                           def __start__():
    76           1          387    387.0      0.0    files = getFileNames('./files')
    77           1            0      0.0      0.0    words = {}
    78           3            0      0.0      0.0    for f in files:
    79           2         3400   1700.0      0.1        content = readFileContent(f)
    80           2      4923513 2461756.5   80.7        words = getWords(content, f, words)
    81       42528        16516      0.4      0.3    for word in (words):
    82       42527       796925     18.7     13.1        words[word] = list2dict(words[word])
    83           1       357948 357948.0      5.9    saveIndex(words)
```

So, let's summarize. We originally had six functions, out of which we discarded two, because they were too trivial or just didn't do anything relevant. Now, we have a total of four functions to review and optimize.

getOffsetUpToWord

Let's first look at the getOffsetUpToWord function, which has a lot of lines for something as simple as adding up the length of the words leading up to the current index. There is probably a more Pythonic way to go about it, so let's try it out.

This function originally comprised 1.4 seconds of the total execution time, so let's try to lower that number by simplifying the code. The adding up of the length of the words can be translated into a reduce expression, as shown here:

```
def getOffsetUpToWord(words, index):
  if(index == 0):
    return 0
  length =  reduce(lambda curr, w: len(w) + curr, words[0:index],
  0)
  return length + index + 1
```

This simplification removes the need for extra time doing variable assignments and lookups. It might not seem like much. However, if we run the profiler again with this new code, the time would go down to 0.9 seconds. There is still an obvious drawback to that implementation: the lambda function. We're dynamically creating a function every time we call `getOffsetUpToWord`. We're calling it 313,868 times, so it would be a good idea to have this function already created. We can just add a reference to it in the reduce expression, as shown here:

```
def addWordLength(curr, w):
  return len(w) + curr

@profile
def getOffsetUpToWord(words, index):
  if not index:
    return 0
  length = reduce(addWordLength, words[0:index], 0)
  return length + index + 1
```

The output should be similar to the following screenshot:

```
Total time: 0.816949 s
File: mapper.py
Function: getOffsetUpToWord at line 13

Line #      Hits         Time  Per Hit   % Time  Line Contents
==============================================================
    13                                           @profile
    14                                           def getOffsetUpToWord(words, index):
    15    313868        80314      0.3      9.8     if not index:
    16     29682         7050      0.2      0.9       return 0
    17    284186       652906      2.3     79.9     length = reduce(addWordLength, words[0:index], 0)
    18    284186        76679      0.3      9.4     return length + index + 1
```

With this minor improvement, the execution time goes down to 0.8 seconds. In the preceding screenshot, we can see that there are still a lot of unwanted hits (and therefore time) spent in the first two lines of the function. This check is unnecessary because the reduce function already defaults to 0. Finally, the assignment to the length variable can be removed, and we can return directly the sum of the length, the index, and the integer 1.

With that, we're left with the following code:

```
def addWordLength(curr, w):
  return len(w) + curr

@profile
def getOffsetUpToWord(words, index):
  return reduce(addWordLength, words[0:index], 0) + index + 1
```

The total execution time for this function went from 1.4 to an amazing 0.67 seconds.

getWords

Let's now move on to the next one: the `getWords` function. It is a pretty slow one. According to the screenshot, the execution of this function adds up to 4 seconds. That's not good. Let's see what we can do about it. First things first, the most expensive (time-consuming) line in this function is the one that calls the `getOffsetUpToWord` function. Since we already optimized that one, the total time of this function is now 2.2 seconds (down from 4 seconds).

That's a pretty decent side effect optimization, but we can still do a bit more for this function. We're using a normal dictionary for the `wordIndexDict` variable, so we have to check whether a key is set before actually using it. Doing that check inside this function takes up about 0.2 seconds. It is not a lot, but an optimization nonetheless. To remove that check, we can use the `defaultdict` class. It is a subclass of the `dict` class, which adds an extra functionality. It sets a default value for when a key doesn't exist. This will remove the need for those 0.2 seconds inside the function.

Another trivial but helpful optimization is the assignment of results to variables. It might seem like a small thing, but doing it 313,868 times will no doubt hurt our timing. So, take a look at these lines:

```
35      313868          1266039         4.0         62.9            line_offset
= getOffsetUpToWord(localWords, idx)
36      313868          108729          0.3         5.4             index =
(line_offset) + currentOffset
37      313868          101932          0.3         5.1
currentOffset = index
```

These lines can be changed into a single line of code, as shown here:

```
currentOffset = getOffsetUpToWord(localWords, idx) +
currentOffset
```

With that, we shaved off another 0.2 seconds. Finally, we're doing a strip operation on every line and then on every word. We can simplify this by calling the `replace` method several times for the entire content when loading the file. This will take care of cleaning up the text we'll be processing and remove added time for lookups and method calls inside the `getWords` function.

The new code looks like this:

```
def getWords(content, filename, wordIndexDict):
    currentOffset = 0
    for line in content:
        localWords = line.split()
        for (idx, word) in enumerate(localWords):
```

```
            currentOffset = getOffsetUpToWord(localWords, idx) +
            currentOffset
            wordIndexDict[word].append([filename, currentOffset])])])])
    return wordIndexDict
```

It only takes 1.57 seconds to run. There is one extra optimization that we might want to look at. It fits this particular case, because the getOffsetUpToWord function is only used in one place. Since this function got reduced to a one-liner, we can just put the one-liner in place of the function call. This one-liner will subtract the lookup time and give us a whopping 1.07 seconds (that's a 0.50 seconds reduction!). This is how the latest version of the function looks:

```
Total time: 1.07077 s
File: mapper.py
Function: getWords at line 21

Line #      Hits         Time  Per Hit   % Time  Line Contents
==============================================================
    21                                             @profile
    22                                             def getWords(content, filename, wordIndexDict):
    23         2            3      1.5      0.0       currentOffset = 0
    24     38858        11974      0.3      1.1       for line in content:
    25     38856        34947      0.9      3.3         localWords = line.split()
    26    352724       120798      0.3     11.3         for (idx, word) in enumerate(localWords):
    27    313868       709905      2.3     66.3           currentOffset = reduce(addWordLength, localWords[0:idx], 0)  + idx + 1 + currentOffset
    28    313868       193142      0.6     18.0           wordIndexDict[word].append([filename, currentOffset])
    29         2            0      0.0      0.0       return wordIndexDict
```

If you'll call the function from several places, this might be an optimization that is not worth having, since it'll hurt the code maintainability. Code maintainability is also an important aspect when developing. It should be a deciding factor when trying to figure out when to stop with the optimization process.

list2dict

Moving on, for the list2dict function, we can't really do much, but we can clean it up to get a more readable code and shave of about 0.1 seconds. Again, we're not doing this strictly for the speed gain, but for the readability gain. We have a chance to use the defaultdict class again and remove the check for a key so that the new code looks like this:

```
def list2dict(list):
    res = defaultdict(lambda: [])
    for item in list:
        res[item[0]].append(item[1])
    return res
```

The preceding code has less lines, is easier to read, and more easy to understand.

saveIndex

Finally, let's take a look at the `saveIndex` function. According to our initial report, this function took 0.23 seconds to preprocess and save the data into the index file. That's a pretty good number already, but we can do a bit better by taking a second look at all the string concatenations we have.

Before saving the data, for every word we generate a string by concatenating several pieces together. In that same loop, we will also reset the `indexLine` and `glue` variables. These actions will add up to a lot of time, so we might want to change our strategy.

This is shown in the following code:

```
def saveIndex(index):
    lines = []
    for word in index:
        indexLines = []
        for filename in index[word]:
            indexLines.append("(%s, %s)" % (filename, ','.join(index[word]
[filename])))
        lines.append(word + "," +  ','.join(indexLines))

    f = open("index-file.txt", "w")
    f.write("\n".join(lines))
    f.close()
```

As you can see in the preceding code, we changed the entire `for` loop. Now, instead of adding the new string to the `indexLine` variable, we appended it into a list. We also removed the map call, which was making sure we were dealing with strings during the `join` call. That `map` was moved into the `list2dict` function, casting the indexes to the string directly while appending them.

Finally, we used the + operator to concatenate strings instead of doing string expansion, which is a more expensive operation. In the end, this function went down from 0.23 seconds to 0.13, giving us a 0.10-second gain in speed.

Summary

To sum things up, we've seen two major profilers used with Python: cProfile, which comes bundled with the language, and line_profiler, which gives us the chance to look at each line of code independently. We also covered some examples of analysis and optimization using them.

In the next chapter, we will look at a set of visual tools that will help us in our job by displaying the same data we covered in this chapter, but in a graphic manner.

3
Going Visual – GUIs to Help Understand Profiler Output

Although we already covered profiling in the previous chapter, the process we went through was like walking in the dark, or at least, in a place with very little light. We kept looking at numbers. Basically, we kept trying to decrease the number of hits, number of seconds, or other similar numbers. However, it was hard to understand how those numbers related to each other based on the representation we had of them.

We couldn't easily see the big blueprint of our system, based off of that output. If our systems would've been even bigger, seeing that blueprint would've been even harder.

Simply because we're human beings and not computers ourselves, we work better when we have some sort of visual aid. In this particular case, our work would benefit if we could better understand how everything is related. To do this, we have tools that provide visual representations of the numbers we saw in the previous chapter. These tools will provide us with much needed help. In turn, we'll be able to locate and fix the bottlenecks of our systems much faster. As an added bonus, we'll have a better understanding of our system.

In this chapter, we'll cover two tools that fall into this category:

- **KCacheGrind / pyprof2calltree**: This combo will provide the ability to transform the output of cProfile into the format required by KCacheGrind, which in turn will help us visualize the information.

- **RunSnakeRun** (http://www.vrplumber.com/programming/ runsnakerun/): This tool will also allow us to visualize and analyze the output from cProfile. It provides square maps and sortable lists to help us in our task.

For each one, we'll go over the basics of installation and UI explanation. Then, we'll grab the examples from *Chapter 2*, *The Profilers*, and reanalyze them based on the output from these tools.

KCacheGrind – pyprof2calltree

The first GUI tool we will see is KCacheGrind. It is a data visualization tool designed to parse and display different formats of profiling data. For our case, we will display the output from cProfile. However, to do this, we'll also need the help from the command-line tool called pyprof2calltree.

This tool is a rebranding of a very popular one called lsprofcalltree.py (https://people.gnome.org/~johan/lsprofcalltree.py). It tries to behave more like the kcachegrind-converter (https://packages.debian.org/en/stable/kcachegrind-converters) package from Debian. We'll use the tool to transform the output from cProfile into something KCacheGrind can understand.

Installation

To install pyprof2calltree, you'll first need to install the pip command-line utility. Then, just use the following command:

```
$ pip install pyprof2calltree
```

Note that all installation steps and instructions are meant for the Ubuntu 14.04 Linux distribution, unless otherwise noted.

Now, for KCacheGrind, the installation is a bit different. The visualizer is part of the KDE desktop environment, so if you already have it installed, chances are that you already have KCacheGrind also. However, if you don't have it (maybe you're a Gnome user), you can just use your package manager and install it. For instance, in Ubuntu, you'd use the following command:

```
$ sudo apt-get install kcachegrind
```

 With this command, you'll probably have to install a lot of packages not directly related to the utility, but to KDE. So, the installation might take some time depending on your Internet connection.

For Windows and OS X users, there is the option of installing the QCacheGrind branch of KCacheGrind, which is already precompiled and can be installed as a binary.

Windows users can download it from `http://sourceforge.net/projects/qcachegrindwin/`, and OS X users can install it using brew:

```
$ brew install qcachegrind
```

Usage

There are two ways to use `pyprof2calltree`: one is from the command line, passing in arguments, and the other one is directly from the **read-eval-print loop(REPL)** (or even from our own scripts being profiled).

The first one (command-line version) comes in very handy when we already have the profiling results stored somewhere. So, with this tool, we can simply run the following command and get the output when needed:

```
$ pyprof2calltree -o [output-file-name] -i input-file.prof
```

There are some optional parameters, which can help us in different cases. Two of them are explained here:

- `-k`: If we want to run KCacheGrind on the output data right away, this option will do it for us
- `-r`: If we don't have the profiling data already saved in a file, we can use this parameter to pass in the Python script we'll use to collect the said data

Now, if you want to use it from the REPL instead, you can simply import either (or both) the `convert` function or the `visualize` function from the `pyprof2calltree` package. The first one will save the data into a file, and the second one will launch KCacheGrind with the output from the profiler.

Here is an example:

```
from xml.etree import ElementTree
from cProfile import Profile
import pstats
xml_content = '<a>\n' + '\t<b/><c><d>text</d></c>\n' * 100 + '</a>'
profiler = Profile()
profiler.runctx(
"ElementTree.fromstring(xml_content)",
locals(), globals())

from pyprof2calltree import convert, visualize
stats = pstats.Stats(profiler)
visualize(stats)        # run kcachegrind
```

This code will call KCacheGrind. It'll show something like what you see in the following screenshot:

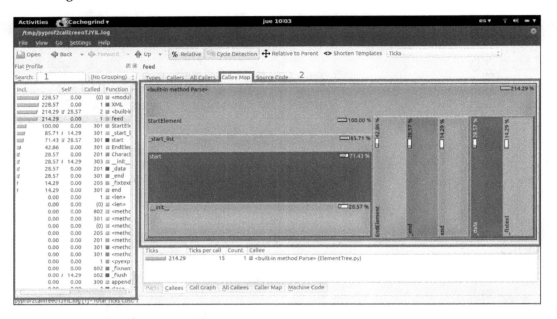

In the preceding screenshot, you can see the list on the left-hand side (**1**) showing some of the numbers we saw in the previous chapter. On the right-hand side (**2**), we've selected one of the tabs, specifically the **Callee Map** tab. It shows a set of boxes, representing the hierarchy of function calls from the one selected on the left-hand side all the way down.

On the list from the left-hand side, there are two columns that we'll want to pay special attention to:

- **Incl. (from Inclusive time) column**: This shows an indicator of how long each function takes in aggregate. This means it adds up the time its code takes plus the time that other functions called by it take. If a function has a high number in this column, it doesn't necessarily mean that the function takes too long. It could mean that the functions called by it do.

- **Self column**: This shows the time spent inside a particular function, without taking into account the ones called by it. So, if a function has a high **Self** value, then it probably means that a lot of time is spent inside it, and it's a good place to start looking for optimization paths.

Another useful view is **Call Graph**, which can be found on the lower-right box once a function is selected on the list. It'll show a representation of the functions that will help explain how each one calls the next one (and how many times). Here is an example from the preceding code:

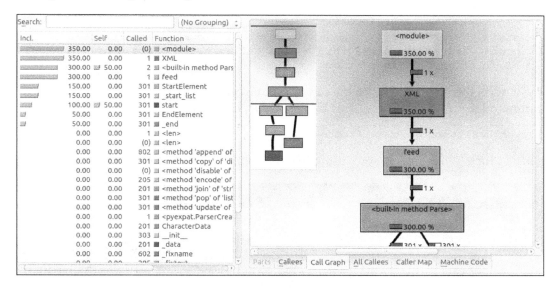

A profiling example – TweetStats

Let's now go back to the examples of *Chapter 2*, *The Profilers*, and tackle them using the pyprof2calltree/kcachegrind combo.

Let's avoid the Fibonacci examples, since they're quite simple and we've been over them already. So, let's jump directly to the code from the TweetStats module. It would read a list of tweets and get some statistics from it. We're not modifying the code. So, for reference, just take a look at it in *Chapter 2*, *The Profilers*.

As for the script using the class and printing the actual stats, we're modifying it to save the stats instead. This is a very simple change as you can see here:

```
import cProfile
import pstats
import sys

from tweetStats import build_twit_stats

profiler = cProfile.Profile()
```

```
profiler.enable()


build_twit_stats()
profiler.create_stats()
stats = pstats.Stats(profiler)
stats.strip_dirs().sort_stats('cumulative').dump_stats('tweet-stats.
prof') #saves the stats into a file called tweet-stats.prof, instead
of printing them into stdout
```

Now, with the stats saved into the `tweet-stats.prof` file, we can use the following command to transform it and start the visualizer all at once:

`$pyprof2calltree -i tweet-stats.prof -k`

This, in turn, will show us something like the following screenshot:

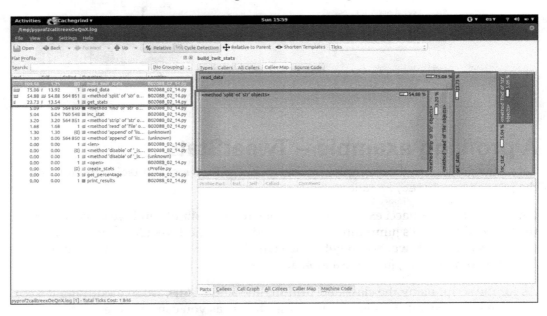

Again, with the **Callee Map** selected for the first function call, we can see the entire map of our script. It clearly shows where the bottlenecks are (biggest blocks on the right-hand side): `read_data`, the `split` method, and the `get_data` function on the far right of the map.

Inside the `get_stats` section of the map, we can see how there are two functions that make up for part of the size: `inc_stat` and `find` from string. We know the first one from seeing the code. This function does very little, so it's entire size will only be due to lookup times accumulated (we're calling it around 760k times after all). The same thing happens for the `find` method. We're calling it way too many times, so the lookup time accumulates and starts to be of notice. So, let's apply a set of very simple improvements to this function. Let's remove the `inc_stat` function and inline it's behavior. Let's also change the `find` method line and use the in operator. The result will look like the one shown in this screenshot: :

That other side of the map changed drastically. Now, we can see that the `get_stats` function no longer calls other functions, so the lookup times were removed. It now only represents 9.45 percent of the total execution time, down from 23.73 percent.

Yes, the preceding conclusions are the same ones we arrived at in the previous chapter, but we did so using a different method. Let's then keep doing the same optimization we did earlier and see how the map changes again:

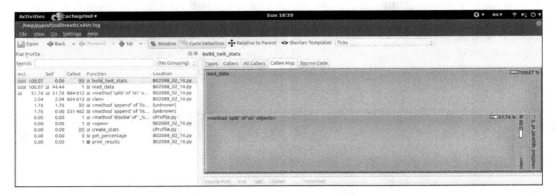

In the preceding screenshot, we see that by selecting the `build_twitt_stats` function (in the list on the left-hand side), the functions that get called are simply methods of the string objects.

Sadly, KCacheGrind isn't showing us the total time of execution. However, the map clearly shows that we've simplified and optimized our code anyway.

A profiling example – Inverted Index

Again, let's get another example from *Chapter 2*, *The Profilers*: the inverted index. Let's update its code in order to generate the stats data and save it into a file so that we can later analyze it with KCacheGrind.

The only thing we need to change is the last line of the file, instead of just calling the `__start__` function. We have the following code:

```
profiler = cProfile.Profile()
profiler.enable()
__start__()
profiler.create_stats()
stats = pstats.Stats(profiler)
stats.strip_dirs().sort_stats('cumulative').dump_stats('inverted-
index-stats.prof')
```

So now, executing the script will save the data into the `inverted-index-stats.prof` file. Later, we can use the following command to start up KCacheGrind:

```
$ pyprof2calltree -i inverted-index-stats.prof -k
```

This is what we will see first:

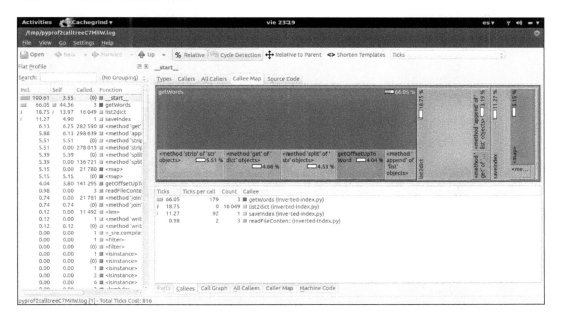

Let's first do a resort of the functions on the left-hand side by the second column (**Self**). So, we can look at the functions that take the longest to execute because of their code (not because of how long the functions it calls take). We will get the following list:

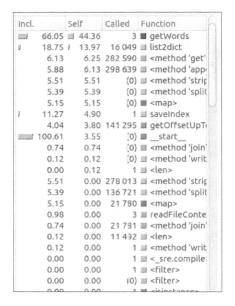

So, according to the preceding list, the two most problematic functions right now are getWords and list2dict.

The first one can be improved in several ways, as follows:

- The wordIndexDict attribute can be changed to be of the defaultdict type, which will remove the if statement checking for an existing index
- The strip statements can be removed from the readFileContent function, simplifying our code here
- A lot of assignments can be removed, so avoid spending milliseconds in them, since we can use the values directly

So, our new getWords function looks like this:

```
def getWords(content, filename, wordIndexDict):
  currentOffset = 0
  for line in content:
    localWords = line.split()
    for (idx, word) in enumerate(localWords):
      currentOffset = getOffsetUpToWord(localWords, idx) +
      currentOffset
      wordIndexDict[word].append([filename, currentOffset])
  return wordIndexDict
```

Now, if we run the stats again, the map and the numbers look a bit different:

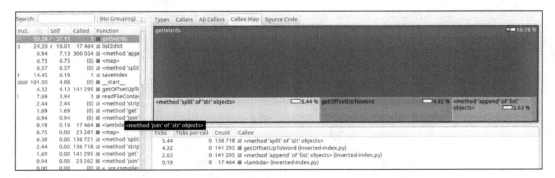

So, our function is now using less time, both overall (**Incl.** column) and inside it (**Self** column). However, there is still another detail we might want to look into before leaving this function alone. The getWords function is calling getOffsetUpToWord a total of **141,295** times, the lookup time spent in there alone, should be enough to merit a review. So, let's see what we can do.

We've already solved this issue in the earlier chapter. We saw that we can reduce the entire `getOffsetUpToWord` function to a one-liner, which we can later write directly inside the `getWords` function to avoid lookup time. With this in mind, let see what our new map looks like:

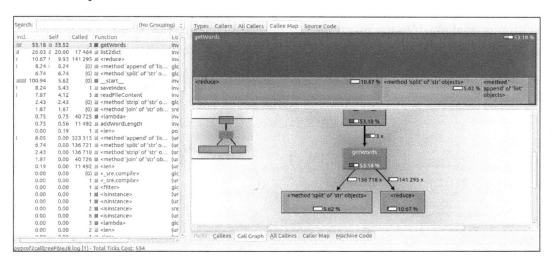

Now, we have increased the overall time, but that's nothing to worry about. It is due to the fact that now we have one function less to spread the timing between, so the number changed for all other functions. However, the one we really care about (the **Self** time) went down, by about 4 percent.

The preceding screenshot also shows the **Call Graph** view, which helps us see that even though we made an improvement, the `reduce` function is still being called over **100,000** times. If you look at the code of the `getWords` function, you would notice we don't really need the `reduce` function. This is because on every call, we're adding up all the numbers we added on the previous call plus one more, so we can simplify this in the following code:

```
def getWords(content, filename, wordIndexDict):
    currentOffset = 0
    prevLineLength = 0
    for lineIndex, line in enumerate(content):
        lastOffsetUptoWord = 0
        localWords = line.split()

        if lineIndex > 0:
            prevLineLength += len(content[lineIndex - 1]) + 1
        for idx, word in enumerate(localWords):
            if idx > 0:
```

```
lastOffsetUptoWord += len(localWords[idx-1])
currentOffset = lastOffsetUptoWord + idx + 1 +
prevLineLength

wordIndexDict[word].append([filename, currentOffset])
```

With this final touch to the functions, the numbers change once again:

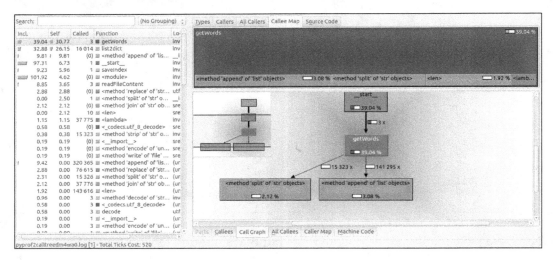

The inclusive amount of time of the function was lowered significantly, so overall, this function now takes less time to execute (which was our goal). The internal time (**Self** column) went down, which is a good thing. This is because it also means that we're doing the same in less time (specially because we know that we're not calling any other function).

RunSnakeRun

RunSnakeRun is yet another GUI tool to help us visualize the profiling output and, in turn, help us make sense of it. This particular project is a simplified version of KCacheGrind. Whereas the latter is also useful for C and C++ developers, RunSnakeRun is specifically designed and written for Python developers.

Earlier, with KCacheGrind, if we wanted to plot the output of cProfile, we needed an extra tool (pyprof2calltree). This time we won't. RunSnakeRun knows how to interpret it and display it, so all we need to do is call it and pass in the path to the file.

The features provided by this tool are as follows:

- Sortable data grid views with fields, such as:
  - function name
  - number of total calls
  - cumulative time
  - filename and line number
- Function-specific information, such as all callers of this function and all callee's of this function
- Square map of the call tree with size proportional to the amount of time spent inside each function

Installation

In order to install this tool, you have to make sure that several dependencies are covered, mainly the following ones:

- Python profiler
- wxPython (2.8 or above) (http://www.wxpython.org/)
- Python (of course!) 2.5 or above, but lower than 3.x

You'll also need to have pip (https://pypi.python.org/pypi/pip) installed in order to run the installation command.

So, make sure you have all these installed before moving forward. If you're in a Debian-based distribution of Linux (say Ubuntu), you can use the following line to make sure you have everything you need (provided you already have Python installed):

```
$ apt-get install python-profiler python-wxgtk2.8 python-setuptools
```

 Windows and OS X users will need to find the correct precompiled binaries for their current OS version for each of the dependencies mentioned earlier.

After that, you can just run this command:

```
$ pip install  SquareMap RunSnakeRun
```

After that, you should be ready to go.

Usage

Now, to quickly show you how to use it, let's go back to previous last example: `inverted-index.py`.

Let's execute that script using the `cProfile` profiler as a parameter and save that output into a file. Then, we can just call `runsnake` and pass it the file path:

```
$ python -m cProfile -o inverted-index-cprof.prof inverted-index.py
$ runsnake inverted-index-cprof.prof
```

This will generate the following screenshot:

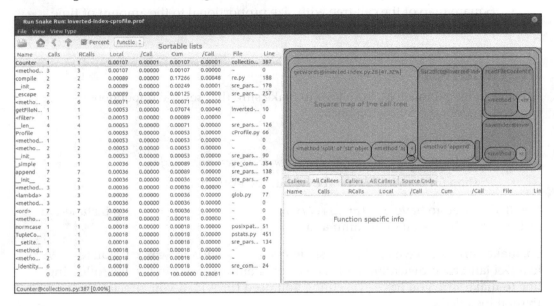

From the preceding screenshot, you can see the three main areas of interest:

- The sortable list, which contains all the numbers returned by `cProfile`
- The function-specific info section, which has several tabs of interest, such as the **Callees**, **Callers** and **Source Code** tabs
- The square map section, which graphically represents the call tree of the execution

A nice little feature that the GUI has is that it'll highlight the related box on the right-hand side if you hover your mouse over a function in the list from the left-hand side. The same thing will happen if you hover over a box on the right-hand side; its corresponding entry in the list will be highlighted.

Profiling examples – the lowest common multiplier

Let's take a look at a very basic, non-practical example of a function in need of serious optimization and what it would look like using this GUI.

Our example function takes care of finding the lowest common multiplier between two numbers. It's a pretty basic example: one you can find all over the Internet. However, it's also a good place to start getting a feel of this UI.

The function's code is as follows:

```
def lowest_common_multiplier(arg1, arg2):
    i = max(arg1, arg2)
    while i < (arg1 * arg2):
        if i % min(arg1,arg2) == 0:
            return i
        i += max(arg1,arg2)
    return(arg1 * arg2)

print lowest_common_multiplier(41391237, 2830338)
```

I'm pretty sure you can spot every single possible optimization just by looking at it, but stay with me. Let's profile this bad boy and load up the resulting output on RunSnakeRun.

So, to run it, use this command:

```
$ python -m cProfile -o lcm.prof lcm.py
```

To start the GUI, use this command:

```
$ runsnake lcm.prof
```

This is what we get:

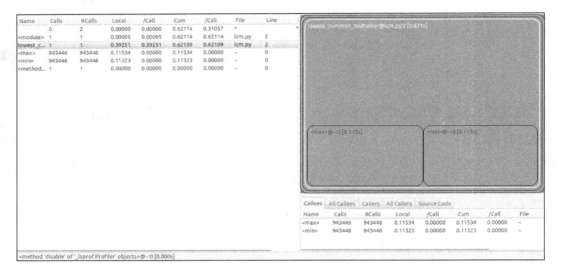

One thing we didn't mention earlier, but that is a nice add-on to the square map, is the fact that next to each box's name, we can see how much time it takes to run that function.

So, at first sight, we can spot several issues already:

- We see that both `max` and `min` functions only take up to 0,228 seconds out of the total 0,621 seconds that our function takes to run. So, there is more to our function than simply max and min.

- We can also see that both `max` and `min` functions are called **943,446** times each. No matter how small the lookup time is, if you call a function almost 1 million times it's going to add up.

Let's perform some obvious fixes to our code and see how it looks again, through the *eyes of the snake*:

```python
def lowest_common_multiplier(arg1, arg2):
    i = max(arg1, arg2)
    _max = i
    _min = min(arg1,arg2)
    while i < (arg1 * arg2):
        if i % _min == 0:
            return i
        i += _max
    return(arg1 * arg2)

print lowest_common_multiplier(41391237, 2830338)
```

You should get something like what's shown in the following screenshot:

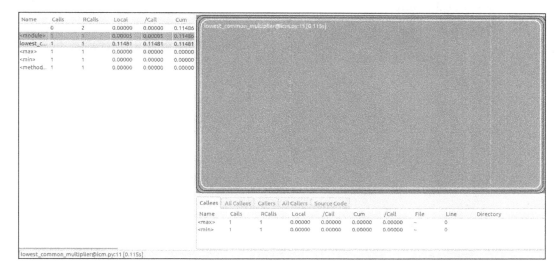

Now, neither `min` nor `max` even register on the square map. This is because we're just only calling them once, and the function went from 0.6 seconds to 0.1 second. This is the power of not doing unnecessary function lookups for you folks.

Now, let's take a look at another, more complex, and thus, interesting function in dire need of optimization.

A profiling example – search using the inverted index

Since the previous chapter, we've been over the code of the inverted index from all possible angles. This is great, since we've analyzed it from several perspectives and using different approaches. However, it would make no sense to also look at it using RunSnakeRun, since this tool is very similar to the one we just tried (KCacheGrind).

So instead, let's use the output of the inverted search script and code ourselves, a search script that will use that output. We will initially shoot for a simple search function that will only look for one single word in the index. The steps are quite straightforward:

1. Load the index in memory.

2. Search for the word and grab the indexing information.

3. Parse the indexing information.

4. For each index entry, read the corresponding file and grab the surrounding string as a result.

5. Print the results.

Here's the initial version of our code:

```
import re
import sys

#Turns a list of entries from the index file into a dictionary indexed
#by words
def list2dict(l):
  retDict = {}
  for item in l:
    lineParts = item.split(',')
    word = lineParts.pop(0)
    data = ','.join(lineParts)
    indexDataParts = re.findall('\((([a-zA-Z0-9\./, ]{2,})\)'
    ,data)
    retDict[word] = indexDataParts
  return retDict


#Load the index's content into memory and parse itdef loadIndex():
  indexFilename = "./index-file.txt"
  with open(indexFilename, 'r') as fh:
    indexLines = []
    for line in fh:
      indexLines.append(line)
    index = list2dict(indexLines)

    return index


#Reads the content of a file, takes care of fixing encoding issues
with utf8 and removes unwanted characters (the ones we didn't want
when generating the index)
def readFileContent(filepath):
    with open(filepath, 'r') as f:
    return [x.replace(",",
    "").replace(".","").replace("\t","").replace("\r","")
    .replace("|","").strip(" ") for x in f.read()
    .decode("utf-8-sig").encode("utf-8").split( '\n' )]
def findMatch(results):
  matches = []
```

```
   for r in results:
     parts = r.split(',')
     filepath = parts.pop(0)
     fileContent = ' '.join(readFileContent(filepath))
     for offset in parts:
       ioffset = int(offset)
       if ioffset > 0:
         ioffset -= 1
       matchLine = fileContent[ioffset:(ioffset + 100)]
       matches.append(matchLine)
   return matches

#Search for the word inside the index
def searchWord(w):
  index = None
  index = loadIndex()
  result = index.get(w)
  if result:
    return findMatch(result)
  else:
      return []

#Let the user define the search word...
searchKey = sys.argv[1] if len(sys.argv) > 1 else None

if searchKey is None: #if there is none, we output a usage message
  print "Usage: python search.py <search word>"
else: #otherwise, we search
  results = searchWord(searchKey)
  if not results:
      print "No results found for '%s'" % (searchKey)
  else:
      for r in results:
      print r
```

To run the code, just run the following command:

```
$ python -m cProfile -o search.prof search.py John
```

The output we will get is similar to the following screenshot (given we have a few books inside the `files` folder):

```
fernandodoglio@glb-l0841:~/workspace/writing/python$ python -m cProfile -o search.prof search.py John
John Burroughs her deepest debt is due To this clear-visioned prophet who has opened the blind eyes
John Burroughs  All the familiar woodpeckers have two characteristics most prominently exemplified i
John Burroughs who calls this bird "the wild Irishman of the flycatchers"   OLIVE-SIDED FLYCATCHER (
John Burroughs calls it "It is not a proud gorgeous strain like the tanager's or the grosbeak's" he
John Burroughs has called the bird the ''bush sparrow"   FOX SPARROW (Passerella ilica) Finch family
John Burroughs "It begins with the words fe-u fe-u fe-u and runs off into trills and quavers like th
John Burroughs in ever-delightful "Wake Robin"; "but no he is doomed to wear the name of some discov
John Burroughs calls him of all our birds "the most native and democratic"  How the robin dominates
John Burroughs is like scarlet "strong intense emphatic" but it is sweet and is more rapidly uttered
John Friese for making the drawings; and to the following for the use of the originals of the illust
John Burroughs  This eBook is for the use of anyone anywhere at no cost and with almost no restricti
John Burroughs  Commentator: Mary E Burt  Posting Date: January 17 2009 [EBook #3163] Release Date:
John Burroughs   With An Introduction  By Mary E Burt  And A Biographical Sketch  CONTENTS   Biogr
John Burroughs's birth A little before the day when the wake-robin shows itself that the observer mi
John Burroughs His books are redolent of the soil and have such "freshness and primal sweetness" tha
John Burroughs's essays I at once foresaw many a ramble with my pupils through the enchanted country
John Burroughs is to live in the woods and fields and to associate intimately with all their little
John Burroughs's essays is much healthier than the over-wrought dramatic action which sets all the n
John Burroughs more than almost any other writer of the time has a prevailing taste for simple words
John Burroughs   MARY E BURT  JONES SCHOOL CHICAGO Sept 1 1887   BIRDS   BIRD ENEMIES   How sure
John the Baptist during his sojourn in the wilderness his divinity school-days in the mountains and
John Burroughs  *** END OF THIS PROJECT GUTENBERG EBOOK BIRDS AND BEES ***  ***** This file should b
```

The output could be improved by highlighting the search term or showing some of the previous words for more context. However, we'll run with it for the time being.

Now, let's see how our code looks when we open the `search.prof` file inside `RunSnakeRun`:

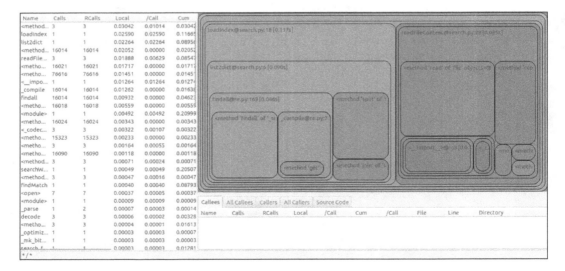

That's a lot of boxes, especially comparing it to our previous example of the lowest common multiplier. However, let's see what insight can be gathered from it at first sight.

The two most time-consuming functions are `loadIndex` and `list2dict`, closely followed by `readFileContent`. We can see this on the left-side column:

- All these functions are actually spending most of their time inside other functions they call. So, their cumulative time is high, but their local time is considerably lower.
- If we sort by local time on the list, we would see that the top five functions are:
    - The `read` method from the file object
    - The `loadIndex` function
    - The `list2dict` function
    - The `findAll` method of the regular expression object
    - And the `readFileContent` function

So, let's first take a look at the `loadIndex` function. Even though most of its time is spent inside the `list2dict` function, we still have one minor optimization to do, which will simplify its code and significantly reduce its local time:

```
def loadIndex():
    indexFilename = "./index-file.txt"
    with open(indexFilename, 'r') as fh:
        #instead of looping through every line to append it into an
        array, we use the readlines method which does that already
        indexLines = fh.readlines()
        index = list2dict(indexLines)
        return index
```

This simple change took the local time of the function from 0.03s down to 0.00002s. Even though it wasn't already a big pain, we both increased its readability and improved its time. So, overall, we did well.

Now, based on the last analysis, we knew that most of the time spent inside this function was actually spent inside another one called by it. So, now that we basically decreased its local time to almost nothing, we need to focus on our next target: `list2dict`.

However, first, let's see how the picture has changed with the simple improvement we did earlier:

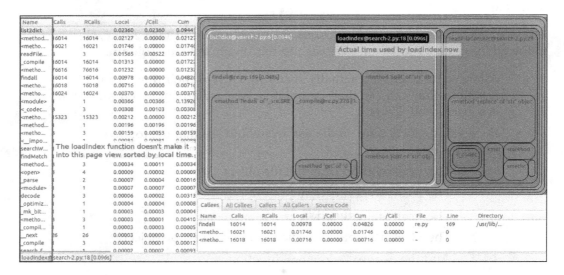

Now, let's move on to `list2dict`. This function is the one in charge of parsing every line of the index file into something we can use later. It will parse every line of the index file, more specifically, into a hash table (or dictionary) indexed by a word, which will make our search be of O(1) in average (read back to *Chapter 1*, *Profiling 101*, if you don't remember what this means) when we search. The values of the dictionary are the path to the actual files and the different offsets where the word is.

From our analysis, we can see that though we spend some time inside the function itself, most of the complexity is inside the regular expression methods. Regular expressions are great for many reasons, but sometimes, we tend to overuse them in cases where using simple `split` and `replace` functions would do. So, let's see how we can parse our data, get the same output without the regular expressions, and see if we can do it in less time: `def list2dict(l):`

```
retDict = {}
for item in l:
  lineParts = item.split(',(')
  word = lineParts[0]
  ndexDataParts = [x.replace(")","") for x in lineParts[1:]]
retDict[word] = indexDataParts
return retDict
```

The code looks cleaner already. There are no regular expressions anywhere (which will help readability sometimes, since not everyone is an expert in reading regular expressions). We have less lines of code. We removed the `join` line, and we even got rid of the nasty `del` line, which was not necessary.

We, however, added a list comprehension line, but this is just a simple `replace` method on every item of the list in one line, that's all.

Let's see what our map looks like now:

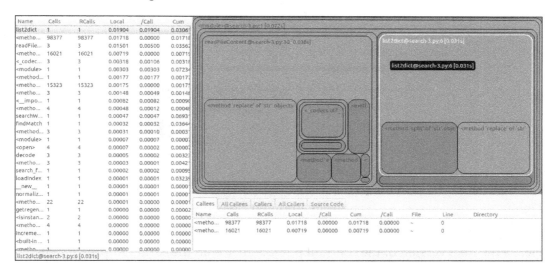

Well, there is definitely a change there. If you compare the last two screenshots, you would notice the box for the `list2dict` function has moved to the right. This means it now takes less time than the `readFileContent` function. Our function's box is also simpler now. The only things inside it are the `split` and the `replace` methods. Finally, in case there was any doubt, let's look at the numbers:

- Local time went down from 0.024s to 0.019s. It makes sense that the local time didn't decrease that much, because we're still doing all the work inside the function. This decrease is mainly due to the absence of the `del` line and the `join` line.

- The total cumulative time decreased considerably. It went down from 0.094s to 0.031s, due to the lack of complex functions (regular expressions) used for the job.

We took the total cumulative time of the function down to a third of what is was. So, it was a good optimization, especially considering that if we had larger indexes, then the time would be much bigger.

The last assumption is not always true. It depends greatly on the type of algorithm being used. However, in our case, since we're looping over all the lines of the index file, we can safely assume it is.

Let's take a quick look at the numbers from the first analysis of the code and the last one so that we can see if there is actually an improvement on the overall time:

Name	Calls	RCalls	Local	/Call	Cum
	0	2	0.00000	0.00000	0.20999
<module>	1	1	0.00492	0.00492	0.20999
searchWord	1	1	0.00049	0.00049	0.20507
loadIndex Original timing			0.02590	0.02590	0.11665

Name	Calls	RCalls	Local	/Call	Cum
	0	2	0.00000	0.00000	0.07234
<module>	1	1	0.00303	0.00303	0.07234
searchW...	1	1	0.00047	0.00047	0.06931
findMatch	1	Final timing	0.00032	0.00032	0.03644

Finally, as you can see, we went from around 0.2 seconds of execution with the original code all the way down to 0.072 seconds.

Here's the final version of the code, all put together with the earlier improvements:

```
import sys

#Turns a list of entries from the index file into a dictionary indexed
#by words
def list2dict(l):
  retDict = {}
  for item in l:
    lineParts = item.split(',(')
  word = lineParts[0]
    indexDataParts = [x.replace(")","") for x in lineParts[1:]]
  retDict[word] = indexDataParts
  return retDict

#Load the index's content into memory and parse it
def loadIndex():
  indexFilename = "./index-file.txt"
  with open(indexFilename, 'r') as fh:
```

```
    #instead of looping through every line to append it into an
    array, we use the readlines method which does that already
    indexLines = fh.readlines()
    index = list2dict(indexLines)
    return index
```

```
#Reads the content of a file, takes care of fixing encoding issues
with utf8 and removes unwanted characters (the ones we didn't want
when generating the index)#
def readFileContent(filepath):
    with open(filepath, 'r') as f:
    return [x.replace(",", "").replace(".","").replace("\t","").
replace("\r","").replace("|","").strip(" ") for x in f.read().
decode("utf-8-sig").encode("utf-8").split( '\n' )]
```

```
def findMatch(results):
  matches = []
  for r in results:
    parts = r.split(',')

    filepath = parts[0]
    del parts[0]
    fileContent = ' '.join(readFileContent(filepath))
    for offset in parts:
      ioffset = int(offset)
      if ioffset > 0:
        ioffset -= 1
      matchLine = fileContent[ioffset:(ioffset + 100)]
      matches.append(matchLine)
  return matches
```

```
#Search for the word inside the index
def searchWord(w):
  index = None
  index = loadIndex()
  result = index.get(w)
  if result:
    return findMatch(result)
  else:
    return []
```

```
#Let the user define the search word...
searchKey = sys.argv[1] if len(sys.argv) > 1 else None

if searchKey is None: #if there is none, we output a usage message
```

```
      print "Usage: python search.py <search word>"
else: #otherwise, we search
    results = searchWord(searchKey)
    if not results:
      print "No results found for '%s'" % (searchKey)
    else:
      for r in results:
      print r
```

Summary

To summarize, in this chapter, we covered two of the most popular and common tools used by Python developers trying to make sense of the numbers returned by profilers such as cProfile. We analyzed the old code under this new light. We even got to analyze some new code.

In the next chapter, we'll start talking about optimization in more detail. We will cover some of the things we've already seen in practice and some recommendations of good practices when profiling and optimizing code.

4
Optimize Everything

The path to mastering performance in Python has just started. Profiling only takes us half way there. Measuring how our program is using the resources at its disposal only tells us where the problem is, not how to fix it. In the previous chapters, we saw some practical examples when going over the profilers. We did some optimization, but we never really explained a lot about it.

In this chapter, we will cover the process of optimization, and to do that, we need to start with the basics. We'll keep it inside the language for now: no external tools, just Python and the right way to use it.

We will cover the following topics in this chapter:

- Memoization / lookup tables
- Usage of default arguments
- List comprehension
- Generators
- ctypes
- String concatenation
- Other tips and tricks of Python

Memoization / lookup tables

This is one of the most common techniques used to improve the performance of a piece of code (namely a function). We can save the results of expensive function calls associated with a specific set of input values and return the saved result (instead of redoing the whole computation) when the function is called with the remembered input. It might be confused with caching, since this is one type of memoization, although this term also refers to other types of optimization (such as HTTP caching, buffering, and so on).

This methodology is very powerful because in practice, it'll turn what should have been a potentially very expensive call into a $O(1)$ function call (for more information about this, refer to *Chapter 1, Profiling 101*) if the implementation is right. Normally, the parameters are used to create a unique key, which is then used on a dictionary to either save the result or obtain it if it's been already saved.

There is, of course, a trade-off to this technique. If we're going to remember the returned values of a memoized function, then we'll be exchanging memory space for speed. This is a very acceptable trade-off, unless the saved data becomes more than what the system can handle.

Classic use cases for this optimization are function calls that repeat the input parameters often. This will assure that most of the time, the memoized results are returned. If there are many function calls, but with different parameters, we'll only store results and spend our memory without any real benefit, as shown in the following image:

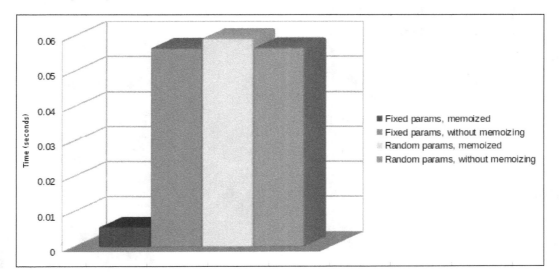

You can clearly see how the blue bar (**Fixed params, memoized**) is clearly the fastest use case, while the others are all similar due to their nature.

Here is the code that generates values for the preceding chart. To generate some sort of time-consuming function, the code will call either the `twoParams` function or the `twoParamsMemoized` function several hundred times under different conditions, and it will log the execution time:

```python
import math

import time

import random

class Memoized:

  def __init__(self, fn):

    self.fn = fn

    self.results = {}

  def __call__(self, *args):

    key = ''.join(map(str, args[0]))

    try:

      return self.results[key]

    except KeyError:

      self.results[key] = self.fn(*args)

    return self.results[key]

@Memoized

def twoParamsMemoized(values, period):

  totalSum = 0

  for x in range(0, 100):
```

```
        for v in values:

            totalSum = math.pow((math.sqrt(v) * period), 4) + totalSum

    return totalSum

def twoParams(values, period):

    totalSum = 0

    for x in range(0, 100):

        for v in values:

            totalSum = math.pow((math.sqrt(v) * period), 4) + totalSum

    return totalSum

def performTest():

    valuesList = []

    for i in range(0, 10):

        valuesList.append(random.sample(xrange(1, 101), 10))

    start_time = time.clock()

    for x in range(0, 10):

        for values in valuesList:

            twoParamsMemoized(values, random.random())

    end_time = time.clock() - start_time

    print "Fixed params, memoized: %s" % (end_time)

    start_time = time.clock()

    for x in range(0, 10):

        for values in valuesList:
```

```
        twoParams(values, random.random())

    end_time = time.clock() - start_time

    print "Fixed params, without memoizing: %s" % (end_time)

    start_time = time.clock()

    for x in range(0, 10):

        for values in valuesList:

            twoParamsMemoized(random.sample(xrange(1,2000), 10),
            random.random())

    end_time = time.clock() - start_time

    print "Random params, memoized: %s" % (end_time)

    start_time = time.clock()

    for x in range(0, 10):

        for values in valuesList:

            twoParams(random.sample(xrange(1,2000), 10),
            random.random())

    end_time = time.clock() - start_time

    print "Random params, without memoizing: %s" % (end_time)

performTest()
```

 The main insight to take from the preceding chart is that, just like with every aspect of programming, there is no silver bullet algorithm that will work for all cases. Memoization is clearly a very basic way of optimizing code, but clearly, it won't optimize anything given the right circumstances.

As for the code, there is not much to it. It is a very simple, non real-world example of the point I was trying to send across. The `performTest` function will take care of running a series of 10 tests for every use case and measure the total time each use case takes. Notice that we're not really using profilers at this point. We're just measuring time in a very basic and ad-hoc way, which works for us.

The input for both functions is simply a set of numbers on which they will run some math functions, just for the sake of doing something.

The other interesting bit about the arguments is that, since the first argument is a list of numbers, we can't just use the `args` parameter as a key inside the `Memoized` class' methods. This is why we have the following line:

```
key = ''.join(map(str, args[0]))
```

This line will concatenate all the numbers from the first parameter into a single value, which will act as the key. The second parameter is not used here because it's always random, which would imply that the key will never be the same.

Another variation of the preceding method is to precalculate all values from the function during initialization (assuming we have a limited number of inputs, of course) initialization and then refer to the lookup table during execution. This approach has several preconditions:

- The number of input values must be finite; otherwise it's impossible to precalculate everything
- The lookup table with all of its values, must fit into memory
- Just like before, the input must be repeated, at least once, so the optimization both makes sense and is worth the extra effort

There are different approaches when it comes to architecting the lookup table, all offering different types of optimizations. It all depends on the type of application and solution that you're trying to optimize. Here is a set of examples.

Performing a lookup on a list or linked list

This solution works by iterating over an unsorted list and checking the key against each element, with the associated value as the result we're looking for.

This is obviously a very slow method of implementation, with a Big O notation of $O(n)$ for both the average and worst case scenarios. Still, given the right circumstances, it could prove to be faster than calling the actual function every time.

In this case, using a linked list would improve the performance of the algorithm over using a simple list. However, it would still depend heavily on the type of linked list it is (doubly linked list, simple linked list with direct access to the first and last elements, and so on).

Simple lookup on a dictionary

This method works using a one-dimensional dictionary lookup, indexed by a key consisting of the input parameters (enough of them create a unique key). In particular cases (like we covered earlier), this is probably one of the fastest lookups, even faster than binary search in some cases with a constant execution time (Big O notation of $O(1)$).

Note that this approach is efficient as long as the key-generation algorithm is capable of generating unique keys every time. Otherwise, the performance could degrade over time due to the many collisions on the dictionaries.

Binary search

This particular method is only possible if the list is sorted. This could potentially be an option depending on the values to sort. Yet sorting them would require extra effort that would hurt the performance of the entire effort. However, it presents very good results, even in long lists (average Big O notation of $O(log\ n)$). It works by determining in which half of the list the value is and repeating until either the value is found or the algorithm is able to determine that the value is not in the list.

To put all of this into perspective, looking at the Memoized class mentioned earlier, it implements a simple lookup on a dictionary. However, this would be the place to implement either of the other algorithms.

Use cases for lookup tables

There are some classic example use cases for this type of optimization, but the most common one is probably the optimization of trigonometric functions. Based on the computing time, these functions are really slow. When used repeatedly, they can cause some serious damage to your program's performance.

This is why it is normally recommended to precalculate the values of these functions. For functions that deal with an infinite domain universe of possible input values, this task becomes impossible. So, the developer is forced to sacrifice accuracy for performance by precalculating a discrete subdomain of the possible input values (that is, going from floating points down to integer numbers).

This approach might not be ideal in some cases, since some systems require both performance and accuracy. So, the solution is to meet in the middle and use some form of interpolation to calculate the required value, based on the ones that have been precalculated. It will provide better accuracy. Even though it won't be as performant as using the lookup table directly, it should prove to be faster than doing the trigonometric calculation every time.

Let's look at some examples of this; for instance, for the following trigonometric function:

```
def complexTrigFunction(x):
    return math.sin(x) * math.cos(x)**2
```

We'll take a look at how simple precalculation won't be accurate enough and how some form of interpolation will result in a better level of accuracy.

The following code will precalculate the values for the function in a range from `-1000` to `1000` (only integer values). Then it'll try to do the same calculation (only for a smaller range) for floating point numbers:

```
import math
import time
from collections import defaultdict
import itertools

trig_lookup_table = defaultdict(lambda: 0)


def drange(start, stop, step):
    assert(step != 0)
    sample_count = math.fabs((stop - start) / step)
    return itertools.islice(itertools.count(start, step),
    sample_count)


def complexTrigFunction(x):
    return math.sin(x) * math.cos(x)**2


def lookUpTrig(x):
```

```
      return trig_lookup_table[int(x)]


for x in range(-1000, 1000):
  trig_lookup_table[x] = complexTrigFunction(x)

trig_results = []
lookup_results = []

init_time = time.clock()
for x in drange(-100, 100, 0.1):
  trig_results.append(complexTrigFunction(x))
print "Trig results: %s" % (time.clock() - init_time)

init_time = time.clock()
for x in drange(-100, 100, 0.1):
  lookup_results.append(lookUpTrig(x))
print "Lookup results: %s" % (time.clock() - init_time)

for idx in range(0, 200):
  print "%s\t%s" % (trig_results [idx], lookup_results[idx])
```

The results from the preceding code will help demonstrate how the simple lookup table approach is not accurate enough (see the following chart). However, it compensates for this with speed, as the original function takes 0.001526 seconds to run while the lookup table only takes 0.000717 seconds.

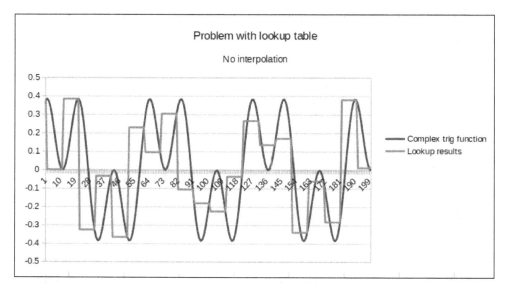

The preceding chart shows how the lack of interpolation hurts the accuracy. You can see how, even though both plots are quite similar, the results from the lookup table execution aren't as accurate as the `trig` function used directly. So, now, let's take another look at the same problem. However, this time, we'll add some basic interpolation (we'll limit the rage of values from -PI to PI):

```python
import math
import time
from collections import defaultdict
import itertools

trig_lookup_table = defaultdict(lambda: 0)

def drange(start, stop, step):
    assert(step != 0)
    sample_count = math.fabs((stop - start) / step)
    return itertools.islice(itertools.count(start, step),
    sample_count)

def complexTrigFunction(x):
  return math.sin(x) * math.cos(x)**2


reverse_indexes = {}
for x in range(-1000, 1000):
  trig_lookup_table[x] = complexTrigFunction(math.pi * x / 1000)


complex_results = []
lookup_results = []

init_time = time.clock()
for x in drange(-10, 10, 0.1):
  complex_results .append(complexTrigFunction(x))
print "Complex trig function: %s" % (time.clock() - init_time)

init_time = time.clock()
factor = 1000 / math.pi
for x in drange(-10 * factor, 10 * factor, 0.1 * factor):
  lookup_results.append(trig_lookup_table[int(x)])
print "Lookup results: %s" % (time.clock() - init_time)

for idx in range(0, len(lookup_results )):
  print "%s\t%s" % (complex_results [idx], lookup_results [idx])
```

As you might've noticed in the previous chart, the resulting plot is periodic (especially because we've limited the range from -PI to PI). So, we'll focus on a particular range of values that will generate one single segment of the plot.

The output of the preceding script also shows that the interpolation solution is still faster than the original trigonometric function, although not as fast as it was earlier:

Interpolation solution	Original function
0.000118 seconds	0.000343 seconds

The following chart is a bit different from the previous one, especially because it shows (in green) the error percentage between the interpolated value and the original one:

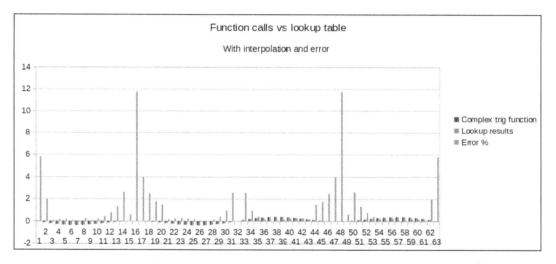

The biggest error we have is around 12 percent (which represents the peaks we see on the chart). However, it's for the smallest values, such as -0.000852248551417 versus -0.00079890550141.6. This is a case where the error percentage needs to be contextualized to see if it really matters. In our case, since the values related to that error are so small, we can ignore that error in practice.

There are other use cases for lookup tables, such as in image processing. However, for the sake of this book, the preceding example should be enough to demonstrate their benefits and the trade-off implied in their usage.

Usage of default arguments

Another optimization technique, one that is contrary to memoization, is not particularly generic. Instead, it is directly tied to how the Python interpreter works.

Default arguments can be used to determine values once at function creation time, instead of at run time.

 This can only be done for functions or objects that will not be changed during program execution.

Let's look at an example of how this optimization can be applied. The following code shows two versions of the same function, which does some random trigonometric calculation:

```python
import math

#original function
def degree_sin(deg):
    return math.sin(deg * math.pi / 180.0)

#optimized function, the factor variable is calculated during function
creation time,
#and so is the lookup of the math.sin method.
def degree_sin(deg, factor=math.pi/180.0, sin=math.sin):
    return sin(deg * factor)
```

 This optimization can be problematic if not correctly documented. Since it uses attributes to precompute terms that should not change during the program's execution, it could lead to the creation of a confusing API.

With a quick and simple test, we can double-check the performance gain from this optimization:

```
import time
import math

def degree_sin(deg):
    return math.sin(deg * math.pi / 180.0) * math.cos(deg * math.pi /
180.0)


def degree_sin_opt(deg, factor=math.pi/180.0, sin=math.sin, cos =
math.cos):
    return sin(deg * factor) * cos(deg * factor)


normal_times = []
optimized_times = []


for y in range(100):
    init = time.clock()
     for x in range(1000):
       degree_sin(x)
    normal_times.append(time.clock() - init)


    init = time.clock()
    for x in range(1000):
      degree_sin_opt(x)
    optimized_times.append(time.clock() - init)


print "Normal function: %s" % (reduce(lambda x, y: x + y, normal_
times, 0) / 100)
print "Optimized function: %s" % (reduce(lambda x, y: x + y,
optimized_times, 0 ) / 100)
```

The preceding code measures the time it takes for the script to finish each of the versions of the function to run its code for a range of 1000. It saves those measurements, and finally, it creates an average for each case. The result is displayed in the following chart:

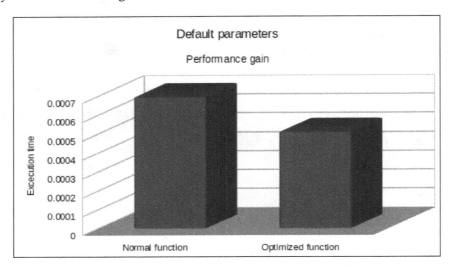

It clearly isn't an amazing optimization. However, it does shave off some microseconds from our execution time, so we'll keep it in mind. Just remember that this optimization could cause problems if you're working as part of an OS developer team.

List comprehension and generators

List comprehension is a special construct provided by Python to generate lists by writing in the way a mathematician would, by describing its content instead of writing about the way the content should be generated (with a classic `for` loop).

Let's see an example of this to better understand how it works:

```
#using list comprehension to generate a list of the first 50 multiples
of 2
multiples_of_two = [x for x in range(100) if x % 2 == 0]

#now let's see the same list, generated using a for-loop
multiples_of_two = []
for x in range(100):
  if x % 2 == 0:
    multiples_of_two.append(x)
```

Now, list comprehension is not meant to replace `for` loops altogether. They are a great help when dealing with loops that, like the earlier one, are creating a list. However, they aren't particularly recommended for those `for` loops that you write because of their side effects. This means you're not creating a list. You're most likely calling a function inside it or doing some other calculation that does not translate into a list. For these cases, a list comprehension expression would actually hurt readability.

To understand why these expressions are more performant than regular `for` loops, we need to do some disassembling and read a bit of bytecode. We can do this because, even though Python is an interpreted language, it is still being translated into bytecode by the compiler. This bytecode is the one that is interpreted. So, using the `dis` module, we can turn that bytecode into something that humans can read, and analyze its execution.

Let's look at the code then:

```
import dis
import timeit

programs = dict(
    loop="""
multiples_of_two = []
for x in range(100):
  if x % 2 == 0:
    multiples_of_two.append(x)
""",
    comprehension='multiples_of_two = [x for x in range(100) if x % 2
== 0]',
)

for name, text in programs.iteritems():
    print name, timeit.Timer(stmt=text).timeit()
    code = compile(text, '<string>', 'exec')
    dis.disassemble(code)
```

That code will output two things:

- The time each piece of code takes to run
- The set of instructions generated by the interpreter, thanks to the `dis` module

Here is a screenshot of how that output would look (in your system, the time might change, but the rest should be pretty similar):

```
comprehension 7.48636889458
  1           0 BUILD_LIST              0
              3 LOAD_NAME               0 (range)
              6 LOAD_CONST              0 (100)
              9 CALL_FUNCTION           1
             12 GET_ITER
      >>     13 FOR_ITER                28 (to 44)
             16 STORE_NAME              1 (x)
             19 LOAD_NAME               1 (x)
             22 LOAD_CONST              1 (2)
             25 BINARY_MODULO
             26 LOAD_CONST              2 (0)
             29 COMPARE_OP              2 (==)
             32 POP_JUMP_IF_FALSE      13
             35 LOAD_NAME               1 (x)
             38 LIST_APPEND             2
             41 JUMP_ABSOLUTE          13
      >>     44 STORE_NAME              2 (multiples_of_two)
             47 LOAD_CONST              3 (None)
             50 RETURN_VALUE
loop 9.42489385605
  2           0 BUILD_LIST              0
              3 STORE_NAME              0 (multiples_of_two)

  3           6 SETUP_LOOP             52 (to 61)
              9 LOAD_NAME               1 (range)
             12 LOAD_CONST              0 (100)
             15 CALL_FUNCTION           1
             18 GET_ITER
      >>     19 FOR_ITER                38 (to 60)
             22 STORE_NAME              2 (x)

  4          25 LOAD_NAME               2 (x)
             28 LOAD_CONST              1 (2)
             31 BINARY_MODULO
             32 LOAD_CONST              2 (0)
             35 COMPARE_OP              2 (==)
             38 POP_JUMP_IF_FALSE      19

  5          41 LOAD_NAME               0 (multiples_of_two)
             44 LOAD_ATTR               3 (append)
             47 LOAD_NAME               2 (x)
             50 CALL_FUNCTION           1
             53 POP_TOP
             54 JUMP_ABSOLUTE          19
             57 JUMP_ABSOLUTE          19
      >>     60 POP_BLOCK
      >>     61 LOAD_CONST              3 (None)
             64 RETURN_VALUE
```

First things first; the output proves that the list comprehension version of the code is, indeed, faster. Now, let's take a closer look at both lists of instructions, side by side, to try to understand them better:

The for loop instructions	Comments	The list comprehension instructions	Comments
BUILD_LIST		BUILD_LIST	
STORE_NAME	The definition of our "multiples_of_ two" list		
SETUP_LOOP			
LOAD_NAME	Range function	LOAD_NAME	Range function
LOAD_CONST	100 (the attribute for the range)	LOAD_CONST	100 (the attribute for the range)
CALL_FUNCTION	Calls range	CALL_FUNCTION	Calls range
GET_ITER		GET_ITER	
FOR_ITER		FOR_ITER	
STORE_NAME	Our temp variable x	STORE_NAME	Our temp variable x
LOAD_NAME		LOAD_NAME	
LOAD_CONST	$X \% 2 == 0$	LOAD_CONST	$X \% 2 == 0$
BINARY_MODULO		BINARY_MODULO	
LOAD_CONST		LOAD_CONST	
COMPARE_OP		COMPARE_OP	
POP_JUMP_IF_FALSE		POP_JUMP_IF_ FALSE	
LOAD_NAME		LOAD_NAME	
LOAD_ATTR	Lookup for the append method	LIST_APPEND	Appends the value to the list
LOAD_NAME	Loads the value of X		
CALL_FUNCTION	Appends the actual value to the list		
POP_TOP			

The for loop instructions	Comments	The list comprehension instructions	Comments
JUMP_ABSOLUTE		JUMP_ABSOLUTE	
JUMP_ABSOLUTE		STORE_NAME	
POP_BLOCK		LOAD_CONST	
LOAD_CONST		RETURN_VALUE	
RETURN_VALUE			

From the preceding table, you can see how the for loop generates a longer list of instructions. The instructions generated by the comprehension code almost looks like a subset of the ones generated by the for loop, with the major difference of how the values are added. For the for loop, they are added one by one, using three instructions (LOAD_ATTR, LOAD_NAME, and CALL_FUNCTION). On the other hand, for the list comprehension column, this is done with one single, optimized instruction (LIST_APPEND).

> This is the reason why when generating a list, the for loop should not be your weapon of choice. This is because the list comprehension you're writing is more efficient and sometimes, even writes more readable code.

That being said, remember to not abuse these expressions by replacing every for loop, even the ones that do other things (side effects). In these cases, list comprehension expressions are not optimized and will take longer than a regular for loop.

Finally, there is one more related consideration to take into account: when generating big lists, comprehension expressions might not be the best solution. This is because they still need to generate every single value. So, if you're generating a list of 100k items, there is a better way. You can use generator expressions. Instead of returning a list, they return a generator object, which has a similar API to what lists have. However, every time you request a new item, that item will be dynamically generated.

The main difference between a generator object and a list object is that the first one doesn't support random access. So, you can't really use the brackets notation for anything. However, you can use the generator object to iterate over your list:

```
my_list = (x**2 for x in range(100))
#you can't do this
```

```
print my_list[1]

#but you can do this
for number in my_list:
    print number
```

Another key difference between lists and generator objects is that you can only iterate once over the latter, while you can do the same as many times as you like over a list. This is a key difference because it will limit the usage of your efficiently generated list. So, take it into account when deciding to go with a list comprehension expression or a generator expression.

This approach might add a little overhead when accessing the values, but it'll be faster when creating the list. Here is a comparison of both list comprehension and generator expressions when creating lists of different lengths:

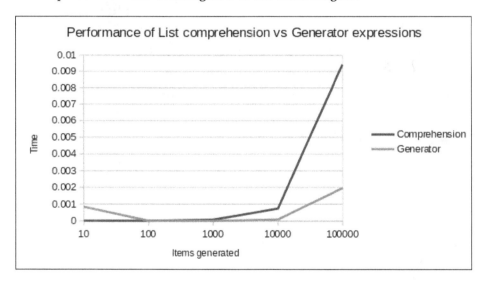

The chart clearly shows that the performance of the generator expressions is better than the list comprehension expressions for lengthier lists. For smaller lists, the list comprehension ones are better.

ctypes

The ctypes library allows the developer to reach under the hood of Python and tap into the power of the C language. This is only possible with the official interpreter (CPython) because it is written in C. Other versions of it, such as PyPy or Jython, do not provide access to this library.

This interface to C can be used to do many things, since you literally have the ability to load pre-compiled code and use it from C. This means you have access to libraries such as `kernel32.dll` and `msvcrt.dll` for Windows systems, and `libc.so.6` for Linux systems.

For our particular case, we'll focus on ways to optimize our code, showing how to load a custom C library and how to load a system library to take advantage of its optimized code. For full details on how to use this library, refer to the official documentation at `https://docs.python.org/2/library/ctypes.html`.

Loading your own custom C library

Sometimes, no matter how many optimization techniques we use on our code, they won't be enough to help us achieve the best possible time. In these cases, we can always write the sensitive code outside our program, in C, compile it into a library, and import it into our Python code.

Let's look at an example of how we can do this and what type of performance boost we are expecting.

The problem to solve is a very simple one, something really basic. We'll write the code to generate a list of prime numbers, from a list of 1 million integers.

The Python code for that could be as follows:

```python
import math
import time


def check_prime(x):
  values = xrange(2, int(math.sqrt(x)))
  for i in values:
    if x % i == 0:
      return False

  return True


init = time.clock()
numbers_py = [x for x in xrange(1000000) if check_prime(x)]
print "%s" % (time.clock() - init)
```

The preceding code is simple enough. Yes, we could easily improve it by changing the list comprehension expression for a generator. However, for the sake of showing the improvement from the C code, let's not do that. Now, the C code is taking 4.5 seconds on average to run.

Let's now write the check_prime function in C, and let's export it into a shared library (.so file):

```c
#include <stdio.h>
#include <math.h>

int check_prime(int a)
{
  int c;
  for ( c = 2 ; c <= sqrt(a) ; c++ ) {
    if ( a%c == 0 )
      return 0;
  }

  return 1;

}
```

To generate the library file, use the following command:

$gcc -shared -o check_primes.so -fPIC check_primes.c

Then, we can edit our Python script to run both versions of the function and compare the times, like this:

```python
import time
import ctypes
import math

check_primes_types = ctypes.CDLL('./check_prime.so').check_prime

def check_prime(x):
  values = xrange(2, int(math.sqrt(x)))
  for i in values:
    if x % i == 0:
      return False

  return True


init = time.clock()
```

```
numbers_py = [x for x in xrange(1000000) if check_prime(x)]
print "Full python version: %s seconds" % (time.clock() - init)

init = time.clock()
numbers_c = [x for x in xrange(1000000) if check_primes_types(x)]
print "C version: %s seconds" % (time.clock() - init)
print len(numbers_py)
```

The preceding code gives the following output:

Full Python version	C version
4.49 seconds	1.04 seconds

The performance boost is pretty good. It has gone from 4.5 seconds down to just 1 second!

Loading a system library

At times, there is no need to code your C function. The system's libraries probably have it for you already. All you have to do is import that library and use the function.

Let's see another simple example to demonstrate the concept.

The following line generates a list of 1 million random numbers, taking 0.9 seconds:

```
randoms = [random.randrange(1, 100) for x in xrange(1000000)]While
this one, takes only 0.3 seconds:
randoms = [(libc.rand() % 100) for x in xrange(1000000)]
```

Here is the full code that runs both lines and prints out the times:

```
import time
import random
from ctypes import cdll


libc = cdll.LoadLibrary('libc.so.6') #linux systems
#libc = cdll.msvcrt #windows systems

init = time.clock()
randoms = [random.randrange(1, 100) for x in xrange(1000000)]
print "Pure python: %s seconds" % (time.clock() - init)

init = time.clock()
randoms = [(libc.rand() % 100) for x in xrange(1000000)]
print "C version : %s seconds" % (time.clock() - init)
```

String concatenation

Python strings deserve a separate portion of this chapter because they're not like strings in other languages. In Python, strings are immutable, which means that once you create one you can't really change its value.

This is a relatively confusing affirmation, since we're used to doing things such as concatenation or replacement on string variables. However, what the average Python developer doesn't realize is that there is a lot more going on behind the curtains than they think.

Since string objects are immutable, every time we do anything to change its content, we're actually creating a whole new string with new content and pointing our variable to that new string. So, we must be careful when working with strings to make sure we actually want to do that.

There is a very simple way to check the preceding scenario. The following code will create a set of variables with the same string (we'll write the string every time). Then, using the id function (which, in CPython, returns the memory address where the value the variable points to is stored), we'll compare them to each other. If strings were mutable, then all objects would be different, and thus, the returned values should be different. Let's look at the code:

```
a = "This is a string"
b = "This is a string"

print id(a) == id(b)  #prints  True

print id(a) == id("This is a string") #prints True

print id(b) == id("This is another String") #prints False
```

As the comments on the code state, the output will be True, True, and False, thus showing how the system is actually reusing the This is a string string every time we write it.

The following image tries to represent the same idea in a more graphical way:

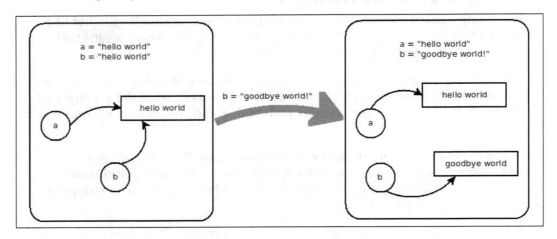

Although we wrote the string twice, internally, both variables are referencing the same block of memory (containing the actual string). If we assign another value to one of them, we would not be changing the string content. We would just be pointing our variable to another memory address.

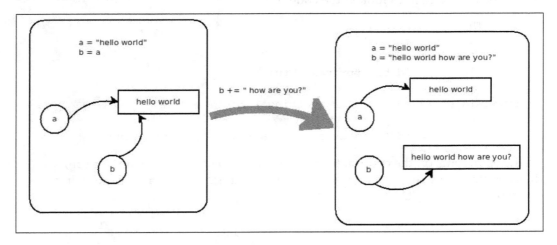

The same thing happens in the preceding case, where we have a variable b pointing directly to variable a. Still, if we try to modify b, we would just be creating a new string once again.

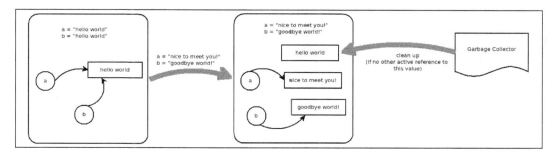

Finally, what happens if we change the value of both our variables from our example? What happens to the `hello world` string stored in memory? Well, if there are no other references to it, the **Garbage Collector** will eventually take care of it, releasing that memory.

That being said, immutable objects are not all that bad. They are actually good for performance if used right, since they can be used as dictionary keys, for instance, or even shared between different variable bindings (since the same block of memory is used every time you reference the same string). This means that the string `hey there` will be the same exact object every time you use that string, no matter what variable it is stored in (like we saw earlier).

With this in mind, think about what would happen for some common cases, such as the following one:

```
full_doc = ""
for word in word_list:
    full_doc += word
```

The preceding code will generate a new string for `full_doc` for every item in the `word_list` list. This is not really efficient memory usage, is it? This is a very common case when we're trying to recreate a string from different parts. There is a better, more memory efficient way of doing it:

```
full_doc = "".join(world_list)
```

The alternative is easier to read, faster to write, and more efficient, both memory and time wise. The following code shows the time each option takes. With the right command, we can also see that the for loop alternative uses a bit more memory:

```python
import time
import sys

option = sys.argv[1]

words =  [str(x) for x in xrange(1000000)]

if option == '1':
  full_doc = ""
  init = time.clock()
  for w in words:
    full_doc += w
  print "Time using for-loop: %s seconds" % (time.clock() - init)
else:
  init = time.clock()
  full_doc = "".join(words)
  print "Time using join: %s seconds" % (time.clock() - init)
```

With the following commands we can execute the script and measure the memory used, using the Linux utility time:

- #for the for-loop version:

  ```
  $ /usr/bin/time -f "Memory: %M bytes" python script.py 1
  ```

- #for the join version:

  ```
  $ /usr/bin/time -f "Memory: %M bytes" python script.py 0
  ```

The output from the for-loop version command is as follows:

```
Time using for-loop: 0.155635 seconds
Memory: 66212 bytes
```

The output from the join version command is as follows:

```
Time using join: 0.015284 seconds
Memory: 66092 bytes
```

The join version clearly takes considerably less time, and the peak memory consumption (measured by the time command) is also less.

The other use case we want to consider when working with strings in Python is a different type of concatenation; it is used when you're only dealing with a few variables, such as the following one:

```
document = title + introduction + main_piece + conclusion
```

You'll end up creating a set of substrings every time the system computes a new concatenation. So a better and more efficient way of doing this is using variable interpolation:

```
document = "%s%s%s%s" % (title, introduction, main_piece, conclusion)
```

Alternatively, it is even better to create substrings using the `locals` function:

```
document = "%(title)s%(introduction)s%(main_piece)s%(conclusion)s" %
locals()
```

Other tips and tricks

The tips mentioned earlier are some of the most common techniques to optimize a program. Some of them are Python specific (such as string concatenation or using ctypes) and others are more generic (such as memoization and lookup tables).

There are still a few more minor tips and tricks specific to Python, which we will cover here. They might not yield a significant boost of speed, but they will shed some more light into the inner workings of the language:

- **Membership testing**: When trying to figure out if a value is inside a list (we use the word "list" generically here, not specifically referencing the type `list`), something such as "a in b", we would have better results using sets and dictionaries (with a lookup time of $O(1)$) than lists or tuples.

- **Don't reinvent the wheel**: Python comes with built-in core blocks that are written in optimized C. There is no need to use hand-built alternatives, since the latter will most likely be slower. Datatypes such as `lists`, `tuples`, `sets`, and `dictionaries`, and modules such as `array`, `itertools`, and `collections.deque` are recommended. Built-in functions also apply here. They'll always be faster to do something such as `map(operator.add, list1, list2)` will always be faster than `map(lambda x, y: x+y, list1, list2)`.

- **Don't forget about deque**: When needing a fixed length array or a variable length stack, lists perform well. However, when dealing with the `pop(0)` or `insert(0, your_list)` operation, try to use `collections.deque`, since it offers fast ($O(1)$) appends and pops up on either end of the list.

- **Sometimes is better not to def**: Calling a function adds a lot of overhead (as we already saw earlier). So, sometimes, in time-critical loops especially, inlining the code of a function, instead of calling that function, will be more performant. There is a big trade-off with this tip, since it could also considerably hurt things such as readability and maintainability. So this should only be done if, in fact, the boost on performance is absolutely required. The following simple example shows how a simple lookup operation ends up adding a considerable amount of time:

```
import time
def fn(nmbr):
    return (nmbr ** nmbr) / (nmbr + 1)
nmbr = 0
init = time.clock()
for i in range(1000):
    fn(i)
print "Total time: %s" % (time.clock() - init)

init = time.clock()
nmbr = 0
for i in range(1000):
  nmbr = (nmbr ** nmbr) / (nmbr + 1)
print "Total time (inline): %s" % (time.clock() - init)
```

- **When possible, sort by the key**: When doing a custom sort on a list, try not to sort using a comparison function. Instead, when possible, sort by the key. This is because the key function will be called only once per item, whereas the comparison function will be called several times per item during the process. Let's see a quick example comparing both methods:

```
import random
import time


#Generate 2 random lists of random elements
list1 = [ [random.randrange(0, 100), chr(random.randrange(32,
122))] for x in range(100000)]
list2 = [ [random.randrange(0, 100), chr(random.randrange(32,
122))] for x in range(100000)]

#sort by string, using a comparison function
init = time.clock()
list1.sort(cmp=lambda a,b: cmp(a[1], b[1]))
print "Sort by comp: %s" % (time.clock() - init) #prints  0.213434

#sort by key, using the string element as key
```

```
init = time.clock()
list2.sort(key=lambda a: a[1])
print "Sort by key: %s" % (time.clock() - init) #prints 0.047623
```

- **1 is better than True**: Python 2.3 `while 1` gets optimized into a single jump, while `while True` does not, thus taking several jumps to complete. This implies that writing `while 1` is more efficient than `while True`, although just like inlining the code, this tip comes with a big trade-off.

- **Multiple assignments are slow but...**: Multiple assignments (`a,b = "hello there", 123`) are generally slower than single assignments. However, again, when doing variable swaps, it becomes faster than doing it the regular way (because we skip the usage and assignment of the temporal variable):

```
a = "hello world"
b = 123
#this is faster
a,b = b, a
#than doing
tmp = a
a = b
b = tmp
```

- **Chained comparisons are good**: When comparing three variables with each other, instead of doing $x < y$ and $y < z$, you can use $x < y < z$. This should prove easier to read (more natural) and faster to run.

- **Using namedtuples instead of regular objects**: When creating simple objects to store data, using the regular class notation, the instances contain a dictionary for attribute storage. This storage can become wasteful for objects with few attributes. If you need to create a large number of those objects, then that waste of memory adds up. For such cases, you can use `namedtuples`. This is a new `tuple` subclass, which can be easily constructed and is optimized for the task. For details on `namedtuples`, check the official documentation at `https://docs.python.org/2/library/collections.html#collections.namedtuple`. The following code creates 1 million objects, both using regular classes and `namedtuples`, and displays the time for each action:

```
import time
import collections

class Obj(object):
  def __init__(self, i):
    self.i = i
    self.l = []
```

```
all = {}

init = time.clock()
for i in range(1000000):
    all[i] = Obj(i)
print "Regular Objects: %s" % (time.clock() - init) #prints
Regular Objects: 2.384832


Obj = collections.namedtuple('Obj', 'i l')

all = {}
init = time.clock()
for i in range(1000000):
    all[i] = Obj(i, [])
print "NamedTuples Objects: %s" % (time.clock() - init) #prints
NamedTuples Objects: 1.272023
```

Summary

In this chapter, we covered several optimization techniques. Some of them are meant to provide big boosts on speed, and/or save memory. Some of them are just meant to provide minor speed improvements. Most of this chapter covered Python-specific techniques, but some of them can be translated into other languages as well.

In the next chapter, we will go over optimization techniques. In particular, we'll cover multi-threading and multiprocessing, and you'll learn when to apply each one.

5
Multithreading versus Multiprocessing

When it comes to optimizing code, concurrency and parallelism are two topics that are rarely left out of the conversation. However, in the case of Python these are topics that are normally used to criticize the language. Critics normally blame the difficulty of using these mechanics versus the actual benefit they bring to the table (which, in some instances, is nonexistent).

In this chapter, we will see that the critics are right some of the time and wrong in other cases. Just like with most tools, these mechanics require certain conditions to work for the developer, instead of working against them. During our tour of the internals of how we can achieve parallelism in Python and on which occasions it is actually worth it, we'll discuss two specific topics:

1. **Multithreading**: This is the most classical approach in trying to achieve true parallelism. Other languages such as C++ and Java provide this feature as well.

2. **Multiprocessing**: Although not as common and with some potentially difficult problems to solve, we'll discuss this feature as a valid alternative to multithreading.

After reading this chapter, you'll fully understand the difference between Multithreading and Multiprocessing. Moreover, you will also understand what a **Global Interpreter Lock (GIL)** is, and how it will affect your decision when trying to pick the right parallelism technique.

Parallelism versus concurrency

These two terms are often used together and even interchangeably, but they are technically two different things. On one side, we have parallelism, which happens when two or more processes can run at the exact same time. This can happen, for instance, in multicore systems, where each process runs on a different processor.

On the other hand, concurrency happens when two or more processes try to run at the same time on top of the same processor. This is usually solved by techniques such as time slicing. However, these techniques do not execute in a truly parallel fashion. It just looks parallel to observers because of the speed at which the processor switches between tasks.

The following diagram tries to illustrate this:

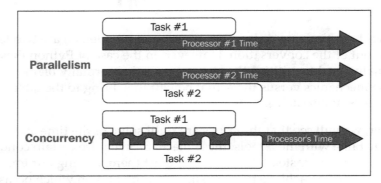

Concurrency, for instance, is a technique used by all modern operating systems. This is because irrespective of the number of processors a computer has, the system alone will probably need to have more processes running at the same time, let alone anything the user might want to do. So, to solve this, the operative system will take care of scheduling time with the processor for each process that requires it. Then, it'll switch context between them, giving each one a slice of time.

Now, with this in mind, how can we achieve either parallelism or concurrency in our Python programs? This is where multithreading and multiprocessing come into play.

Multithreading

Multithreading is the ability of a program to run multiple threads within the context of the same program. These threads share the process's resources and allow multiple actions to run in the concurrent mode (for single processor systems) and in the parallel mode (for multicore systems).

Structuring your program to utilize these threads is not an easy task. However, it comes with some very interesting benefits:

- **Responsiveness**: In single-threaded programs, executing a long running task might cause the program to appear to freeze. Thanks to multithreading and by moving such code into a worker thread, the program can remain responsive while concurrently executing the long running task.

- **Faster execution**: In multicore processors or multiprocessor systems, multithreading can be used to improve the program's performance by achieving true parallelism.

- **Lower resource consumption**: Using threads, a program can serve many requests using the resources from the original process.

- **Simplified sharing and communication**: Since threads already share the same resources and memory space, communication between them is much simpler than interprocess communication.

- **Parallelization**: Multicore or multiprocessor systems can be used to leverage multithreading and run each thread independently. **Compute Unified Device Architecture (CUDA)** from Nvidia (http://www.nvidia.com/object/cuda_home_new.html) or OpenCL from Khronos Group (https://www.khronos.org/opencl/) are GPU-computing environments that utilize from dozens to hundreds of processors to run tasks in parallel.

There are also some drawbacks of multithreading:

- **Thread synchronization**: Since threads can potentially work on the same data, you will need to implement some sort of mechanics to prevent race conditions (causing corrupted data reads).

- **Crash due to problematic thread**: Although it might seem independent, a single problematic thread acting up and performing an invalid action can crash the entire process.

- **Deadlocks**: This is a common problem associated with working with threads. Normally, when a thread needs a resource, it will lock it until it is done with it. A deadlock occurs when one thread enters a wait state, waiting for a second thread to release its resources but the second thread is, in turn, waiting for the first one to release its locked ones.

Normally, this technique should be enough to achieve parallelism on multiprocessor systems. However, the official version of Python (CPython) has a limitation called GIL. This GIL prevents multiple native threads from running Python's bytecode at once, which effectively trumps parallelism. If you have a four-processor system, your code would not run at 400 percent. Instead, it would just run at 100 percent or a bit slower actually, because of the extra overhead from threading.

Note that the GIL is not an invention only of Python (or CPython). Other programming languages also have a GIL, such as Ruby's official implementation Ruby MRI or even OCaml (`https://ocaml.org/`).

A GIL is necessary because the memory management in CPython is not thread safe. So, by forcing everything to run serially, it makes sure that nothing corrupts the memory. It is also faster for single-threaded programs and simplifies the creation of C extensions, because they don't have to take multithreading into account.

There are, however, some ways around the GIL. For instance, since it only prevents threads from running Python's bytecode at the same time, you could potentially code your tasks in C and have Python just as a wrapper for that code. The GIL would not stop the C code from running all threads concurrently in this case.

Another example where the GIL will not affect the performance would be a network server, which spends most of its time reading packets off the network. In this case, the added concurrency will allow more packets to be serviced, even if there is no real parallelism. This effectively boosts the performance of our program (it can serve a lot more clients per second), but it does not affect its speed, as every task takes the same amount of time

Threads

Now, let's talk a bit about threads in Python in order to understand how to use them. They are composed of a beginning, an execution sequence, and a conclusion. There is also an instruction pointer, which keeps track of where a thread is currently running within the thread's context.

That pointer can be pre-empted or interrupted in order to stop the thread. Alternatively, it can also be put on hold temporarily. This basically means putting the thread to sleep.

In order to work with threads in Python, we have the following two options:

- **The thread module**: This provides some limited ability to work with threads. It's simple to use, and for small tasks, it adds little overhead.
- **The threading module**: This is newer and included in Python since version 2.4. It provides a more powerful and higher level support for threads.

Creating a thread with the thread module

Although we'll focus on the threading module, we'll quickly show an example of how to use this module for the simpler times, when not a lot of work is required from your script.

The thread module (https://docs.python.org/2/library/thread.html) provides the start_new_thread method. We can pass it in the following parameters:

- We can pass it in a function that will contain the actual code to run. Once this function returns, the thread will be stopped.

- We can pass it in a tuple of arguments. This list will be passed to the function.

- Finally, we can pass it in an optional dictionary of named arguments.

Let's see an example of all the preceding parameters:

```python
#!/usr/bin/python

import thread
import time

# Prints the time 5 times, once every "delay" seconds
def print_time( threadName, delay):
    count = 0
    while count < 5:
        time.sleep(delay)
        count += 1
        print "%s: %s" % ( threadName, time.ctime(time.time()) )

# Create two threads as follows
try:
    thread.start_new_thread( print_time, ("Thread-1", 2, ) )
    thread.start_new_thread( print_time, ("Thread-2", 4, ) )
except:
    print "Error: unable to start thread"

# We need to keep the program working, otherwise the threads won't
live

while True:
    pass
```

The preceding code prints the following output:

```
Thread-1: Thu Mar 26 16:51:52 2015
Thread-1: Thu Mar 26 16:51:54 2015
Thread-2: Thu Mar 26 16:51:54 2015
Thread-1: Thu Mar 26 16:51:56 2015
Thread-2: Thu Mar 26 16:51:58 2015
Thread-1: Thu Mar 26 16:51:58 2015
Thread-1: Thu Mar 26 16:52:00 2015
Thread-2: Thu Mar 26 16:52:02 2015
Thread-2: Thu Mar 26 16:52:06 2015
Thread-2: Thu Mar 26 16:52:10 2015
```

The preceding code is simple enough, and the output clearly shows how both threads are actually running concurrently. The interesting thing about this is that in the code, the `print_time` function itself has an inside loop. If we were to run this function twice serially, then it would last 5 * delay seconds each time we call it.

However, using threads and without having to change anything, we're running the loop twice concurrently.

This module also provides other threading primitives that can come in handy. Here is an example:

```
interrupt_main
```

This method sends a keyboard interrupt exception to the main thread. This, effectively, is like hitting *CTRL+C* on your program while running. If not caught, the thread that sent the signal would terminate the program.

exit

This method exits the thread silently. It is a good way to terminate a thread without affecting anything else. Let's assume that we changed our `print_time` function into the following lines of code:

```python
def print_time( threadName, delay):
    count = 0
    while count < 5:
        time.sleep(delay)
        count += 1
        print "%s: %s" % ( threadName, time.ctime(time.time()) )
        if delay == 2 and count == 2:
        thread.exit()
```

In this case, the output would be as follows:

```
Thread-1: Fri Mar 27 10:53:41 2015
Thread-2: Fri Mar 27 10:53:43 2015
Thread-1: Fri Mar 27 10:53:43 2015
Thread-2: Fri Mar 27 10:53:47 2015
Thread-2: Fri Mar 27 10:53:51 2015
Thread-2: Fri Mar 27 10:53:55 2015
Thread-2: Fri Mar 27 10:53:59 2015
```

After these two excecutions this thread exits.

The `allocate_lock` method returns a lock for the threads to use. The lock will help the developer protect sensitive code and make sure that there are no race conditions during execution.

The lock objects returned have these three simple methods:

- `acquire`: This basically acquires the lock for the current thread. It accepts an optional integer parameter. If it is zero, the lock would be acquired only if it can be acquired immediately, without waiting. If it's non-zero, the lock would be acquired unconditionally (like when you omit the parameter). This means that if the thread needs to wait to acquire the lock, it would.

- `release`: This will release the lock for the next thread to acquire it.

- `locked`: This would return TRUE if the lock is acquired by some thread. Otherwise, it would be FALSE.

Here is a very basic example of how locking can help multithreaded code. The following code increments a global variable using 10 threads. Each one will add one thread. So, by the end, we should have 10 threads in that global variable:

```python
#!/usr/bin/python

import thread
import time

global_value = 0

def run( threadName ):
    global global_value
    print "%s with value %s" % (threadName, global_value)
    global_value = global_value + 1


for i in range(10):
```

```
thread.start_new_thread( run, ("Thread-" + str(i), ) )

# We need to keep the program working, otherwise the threads won't
live
while 1:
    pass
```

Here is the output of the preceding code:

```
Thread-1 with value 0Thread-3 with value 0
 Thread-6 with value 0
Thread-8 with value 0

Thread-4 with value 0Thread-0 with value 1
Thread-5 with value 2

 Thread-2 with value 0
Thread-7 with value 0
Thread-9 with value 1
```

Not only are we correctly incrementing the value of the global variable (we only got up to 2), but we are also having issues printing out the strings. In some cases, we have two strings in the same line, when they should each occupy one. This is because when two strings existed in the same line, both threads tried to print at the same time. At that time, the current line to print on was the same in both cases.

The same occurrence repeats for the global value. When threads 1, 3, 6, 8, 4, 2, and 7 read the value of the global variable in order to add 1, the value was 0 (which is what they each copied to the local_value variable). We need to make sure that the code that copies the value, increments it, and prints it out is protected (inside a lock) so that no two threads can run it at the same time. To accomplish this, we'll use two methods for the Lock object: acquire and release.

Use the following lines of code:

```
#!/usr/bin/python

import thread
import time

global_value = 0

def run( threadName, lock ):
    global global_value
    lock.acquire()
    local_copy = global_value
    print "%s with value %s" % (threadName, local_copy)
```

```
        global_value = local_copy + 1
        lock.release()

lock = thread.allocate_lock()

for i in range(10):
    thread.start_new_thread( run, ("Thread-" + str(i), lock) )

# We need to keep the program working, otherwise the threads won't
live
while 1:
    pass
```

Now, the output makes more sense:

```
Thread-1 with value 0
Thread-6 with value 1
Thread-7 with value 2
Thread-3 with value 3
Thread-5 with value 4
Thread-2 with value 5
Thread-4 with value 6
Thread-0 with value 7
Thread-9 with value 8
Thread-8 with value 9
```

The output now makes more sense, the format got fixed, and we successfully incremented the value of our variable. Both fixes are due to the locking mechanics. Regarding the code, to increment the value of global_value, the lock is preventing other threads (those which have not yet acquired the lock) from executing that part of the code (reading its value into a local variable and incrementing it). So, while the lock is active, only the thread that acquired it will be able to run those lines. After the lock has been released, the next thread in line will do the same. The preceding line of code returns the current threads identified:

```
get_ident
```

This is a non-zero integer with no direct meaning other than identifying the current thread between the lists of active ones. This number can be recycled after a thread dies or exits, so it is not unique during the lifetime of the program. The following code sets or returns the thread stack size used when creating new threads:

```
stack_size
```

This supports an optional argument ("this" being the size to set for the stack). This size must either be 0 or at least 32.768 (32 Kb). Depending on the system, there might be other restrictions to the number or even to setting the stack size. So, check with your OS's manual before trying to use this method.

 Although it is not the target version of this book, in Python 3, this module has been renamed to _thread.

Working with the threading module

This is the current and recommended way to work with threads in Python. This module provides a better and higher level interface for that. It also adds complexity to our code, since the simplicity of the _thread module will not be available now.

For this case, we can loosely quote Uncle Ben and say:

With great power comes great complexity.

Jokes apart, the threading module encapsulates the concept of thread inside a class, which we're required to instantiate to be able to use.

We can create a subclass of the Thread class (https://docs.python.org/2/library/thread.html) provided by the module (this is normally the preferred way). Alternatively, we could even instantiate that class directly if we want to do something very simple. Let's see how the preceding example would translate using the threading module:

```python
#!/usr/bin/python

import threading

global_value = 0

def run( threadName, lock ):
    global global_value
    lock.acquire()
    local_copy = global_value
    print "%s with value %s" % (threadName, local_copy)
    global_value = local_copy + 1
    lock.release()

lock = threading.Lock()

for i in range(10):
```

```
t = threading.Thread( target=run, args=("Thread-" + str(i),
lock) )
t.start()
```

For more complex things, we might want to create our own thread classes in order to better encapsulate its behavior.

When using the subclass approach, there are a few things you need to take into account when writing your own classes:

- They need to extend the `threading.Thread` class
- They need to overwrite the `run` method and, optionally, the `__init__` method
- If you overwrite the constructor, make sure to call the parent's class constructor (`Thread.__init__`) as the first action you take
- The thread will stop when the `run` method stops or throws an unhandled exception, so plan your method with this in mind
- You can name your thread with the `name` argument on its constructor method

Although you'll have to overwrite the `run` method, which will contain the main logic of the thread, you will not be in control of when that method is called. Instead, you will call the `start` method, which, in turn, will create a new thread and call the `run` method with that thread as context.

Let's now look at a simple example of a very common pitfall of working with threads:

```python
import threading
import time


class MyThread(threading.Thread):

  def __init__(self, count):
    threading.Thread.__init__(self)
    self.total = count

  def run(self):

    for i in range(self.total):
      time.sleep(1)
      print "Thread: %s - %s" % (self.name, i)


t = MyThread(4)
```

```
t2 = MyThread(3)

t.start()
t2.start()

print "This program has finished"
```

The output of that code is as follows:

```
This program has finished
Thread: Thread-2 - 0
 Thread: Thread-1 - 0
Thread: Thread-2 - 1
 Thread: Thread-1 - 1
Thread: Thread-2 - 2
 Thread: Thread-1 - 2
Thread: Thread-1 - 3
```

As you can see highlighted in the preceding screenshot, the program is sending the exit message before anything else. In this case, it's not a big issue. However, it would be a problem if we had something like this:

```
#....
f = open("output-file.txt", "w+")
t = MyThread(4, f)
t2 = MyThread(3, f)

t.start()
t2.start()
f.close() #close the file handler
print "This program has finished"
```

 Note that the preceding code will fail, because it will close the file handler before any thread tries to use it in any way. If we want to avoid this type of issue, we need to use the join method, which will halt the calling thread until the target thread has completed execution.

In our case, if we use the join method from the main thread, it would make sure that the program does not continue with the main chain of commands until both threads complete execution. We need to make sure we use the join method on the threads after both have started. Otherwise, we could end up running them serially:

```
#...
t.start()
t2.start()
#both threads are working, let's stop the main thread
```

```
t.join()
t2.join()
f.close() #now that both threads have finished, lets close the file
handler
print "This program has finished"
```

This method also accepts an optional argument: a timeout (a float or None) in seconds. However, the join method always returns None. So, to find out whether the operation indeed timed out, we need to check whether the thread is still alive (with the isAlive method) after the join method returns. If the thread is alive, then the operation timed out.

Let's now see another example of a simple script to check the status code of a list of sites. This script requires just a few lines of code to iterate over the list and collect the status code returned:

```
import urllib2

sites = [
  "http://www.google.com",
  "http://www.bing.com",
  "http://stackoverflow.com",
  "http://facebook.com",
  "http://twitter.com"
]

def check_http_status(url):
  return urllib2.urlopen(url).getcode()


http_status = {}
for url in sites:
  http_status[url] = check_http_status(url)


for  url in http_status#:
  print "%s: %s" % (url, http_status[url])
```

If you run the preceding code with the time command-line tool on Linux, you could also get the time it takes to execute:

```
$time python non_threading_httpstatus.py
```

The output is as follows:

```
http://www.google.com: 200
http://facebook.com: 200
http://stackoverflow.com: 200
http://www.bing.com: 200
http://twitter.com: 200

real    0m3.936s
user    0m0.060s
sys     0m0.018s
```

Now, looking at the code and with what we've seen so far, a clear optimization would be to turn the IO-bound function (check_http_status) into a thread. This way, we can concurrently check the status for all sites, instead of waiting for each request to finish before processing the next one:

```python
import urllib2
import threading


sites = [
  "http://www.google.com",
  "http://www.bing.com",
  "http://stackoverflow.com",
  "http://facebook.com",
  "http://twitter.com"
]

class HTTPStatusChecker(threading.Thread):

  def __init__(self, url):
    threading.Thread.__init__(self)
    self.url = url
    self.status = None

  def getURL(self):
    return self.url

  def getStatus(self):
    return self.status

  def run(self):
```

```
        self.status = urllib2.urlopen(self.url).getcode()


threads = []
for url in sites:
    t = HTTPStatusChecker(url)
    t.start() #start the thread
    threads.append(t)


#let the main thread join the others, so we can print their result
after all of them have finished.
for t in threads:
    t.join()

for  t in threads:
    print "%s: %s" % (t.url, t.status)
```

Running the new script with time will produce the following result:

$time python threading_httpstatus.py

We will get the following output:

```
http://www.google.com: 200
http://www.bing.com: 200
http://stackoverflow.com: 200
http://facebook.com: 200
http://twitter.com: 200

real    0m1.576s
user    0m0.068s
sys     0m0.016s
```

Clearly, the threaded alternative is faster. In our case, it is almost three times faster, which is an amazing improvement.

Interthread communication with events

Although threads are normally thought of as individual or parallel workers, sometimes, it is useful to allow them to communicate with each other.

To achieve this, the threading module provides the event construct (https://docs.python.org/2/library/threading.html#event-objects). It contains an internal flag, and caller threads can either use set() or clear().

The `Event` class has a very simple interface. Here are the methods provided within the class:

- `is_set`: this would return `True` if the internal flag of the event is set.
- `set`: this sets the internal flag to `True`. It awakens all threads waiting for this flag to be set. Threads calling `wait()` will no longer be blocked.
- `clear`: this resets the internal flag. Any thread calling the `wait()` method will become blocked until `set()` is called again.
- `wait`: this blocks the calling thread until the internal flag of the event is set. This method accepts an optional argument for a timeout. If it is specified and different from none, then the thread would be blocked only by that timeout.

Let's see a simple example of using events to communicate between two threads so that they can take turns printing out to a standard output. Both threads will share the same event object. One will set it on every iteration of the `while` loop, and the other would clear it if it's set. On every action (`set` or `clear`), they'll print the right letter:

```python
import threading
import time


class ThreadA(threading.Thread):

    def __init__(self, event):
        threading.Thread.__init__(self)
        self.event = event


    def run(self):
        count = 0
        while count < 5:
            time.sleep(1)
            if self.event.is_set():
                print "A"
                self.event.clear()
            count += 1

class ThreadB(threading.Thread):

    def __init__(self, evnt):
        threading.Thread.__init__(self)
```

```
        self.event = evnt


    def run(self):
      count = 0
      while count < 5:
        time.sleep(1)
        if not self.event.is_set():
          print "B"
          self.event.set()
        count += 1


  event = threading.Event()

  ta = ThreadA(event)
  tb = ThreadB(event)

  ta.start()
  tb.start()
```

In conclusion, the following table shows when to use multithreading and when not to:

Use threads	Don't use threads
For heavy IO-bound scripts	To optimize scripts that are heavily CPU bound
When parallelism can be replaced by concurrency	For programs that must take advantage of multicore systems
For GUI development	

Multiprocessing

Multithreading in Python fails to achieve real parallelism, thanks to the GIL, as we saw earlier. Thus, some types of applications will not see a real benefit from using this module.

Instead, Python provides an alternative to multithreading called multiprocessing. In multiprocessing, threads are turned into individual subprocesses. Each one will run with its own GIL (which means there are no limitations on the number of parallel Python processes that can run at the same time).

To clarify, threads are all part of the same process, and they share the same memory, space, and resources. On the other hand, processes don't share memory space with their spawning parent, so it might be more complicated for them to communicate with each other.

This approach comes with advantages and disadvantages over the multithreading alternative:

Advantages	Disadvantages
Takes advantage of multicore systems	Larger memory footprint
Separate memory space removes race conditions from the equation	Harder to share mutable data between processes
Child processes are easily interruptible (killable)	**Interprocess communication (IPC)** is harder than with threads
Avoids the GIL limitation (although only in the case of CPython)	

Multiprocessing with Python

The `multiprocessing` module (`https://docs.python.org/2/library/multiprocessing.html`) provides the `Process` class, which, in turn, has an API similar to the `threading.Thread` class. So, migrating code from multithreading to multiprocessing is not as difficult as one might think, because the basic structure of your code would remain the same.

Let's look at a quick example of how we might structure a multiprocessing script:

```
#!/usr/bin/python

import multiprocessing

def run( pname ):
  print pname

for i in range(10):
  p = multiprocessing.Process(target=run, args=("Process-" +
  str(i), ))
  p.start()
  p.join()
```

The preceding code is a basic example, but it shows just how similar to multithreading the code can be.

Note that on Windows systems, you will need to add an extra check to make sure that when the subprocesses include the main code, it would not be executed again. To clarify, the main code should look like this (if you plan to run it on Windows):

```python
#!/usr/bin/python

import multiprocessing

def run( pname ):
  print pname

if __name__ == '__main__':
  for i in range(10):
    p = multiprocessing.Process(target=run,
    args=("Process-" + str(i), ))
    p.start()
    p.join()
```

Exit status

When each process is finished (or terminated), it has an exit code, which is a number representing the result of the execution. This number might either indicate that the process finished correctly, incorrectly, or that it was terminated by another process.

To be more precise:

- A code equal to 0 means there was no problem at all
- A code higher than 0 means the process failed and exited with that code
- A code lower than 0 means it was killed with a -1 * exit_code signal

The following code shows how to read the exit code and how it is set, depending on the outcome of the task:

```python
import multiprocessing
import time

def first():
  print "There is no problem here"

def second():
  raise RuntimeError("Error raised!")

def third():
  time.sleep(3)
```

```
    print "This process will be terminated"

workers = [ multiprocessing.Process(target=first), multiprocessing.
Process(target=second), multiprocessing.Process(target=third)]

for w in workers:
  w.start()

workers[-1].terminate()

for w in workers:
  w.join()

for w in workers:
  print w.exitcode
```

The output of this script is shown in the following screenshot:

Notice how the print property from the third worker is never executed. This is because that process is terminated before the sleep method finishes. It is also important to note that we're doing two separate for loops over the three workers: one to start them and the second one to join them using the join() method. If we were, for instance, to execute the join() method while starting each subprocess, then the third subprocess would not fail. In fact, it would return an exit code of zero (no problem), because as with multithreading, the join() method will block the calling process until the target one finishes.

Process pooling

This module also provides the `Pool` class (`https://docs.python.org/2/library/multiprocessing.html#module-multiprocessing.pool`), which represents a pool of worker processes that facilitate different ways to execute a set of tasks in subprocesses.

The main methods provided by this class are:

- `apply`: This executes a function in a separate subprocess. It also blocks the calling process until the called function returns.

- `apply_async`: This executes a function in a separate subprocess, asynchronously, which means that it'll return immediately. It returns an `ApplyResult` object. To get the actual returned value, you need to use the `get()` method. This action will be blocked until the asynchronously executed function finishes.

- `map`: This executes a function for a list of values. It is a blocking action, so the returned value is the result of applying the function to each value of the list.

Each one of them provides a different way of iterating over your data, be it asynchronously, synchronously, or even one by one. It all depends on your needs.

Interprocess communication

Now, getting the processes to communicate with each other is not, as we already mentioned, as easy as with threads. However, Python provides us with several tools to achieve this.

The `Queue` class provides a thread-safe and process-safe **first in first out** (FIFO) (`https://docs.python.org/2/library/multiprocessing.html#exchanging-objects-between-processes`) mechanism to exchange data. The `Queue` class provided by the multiprocessing module is a near clone of `Queue.Queue`, so the same API can be used. The following code shows an example of two processes interacting through `Queue`:

```
from multiprocessing import Queue, Process
import random

def generate(q):
  while True:
    value = random.randrange(10)
    q.put(value)
    print "Value added to queue: %s" % (value)

def reader(q):
```

```
    while True:
      value = q.get()
      print "Value from queue: %s" % (value)


queue = Queue()
p1 = Process(target=generate, args=(queue,))
p2 = Process(target=reader, args=(queue,))

p1.start()
p2.start()
```

Pipes

Pipes provide (`https://docs.python.org/2/library/multiprocessing.html#exchanging-objects-between-processes`) a bidirectional channel of communication between two processes. The `Pipe()` function returns a pair of connection objects, each representing one side of the pipe. Each connection object has both a `send()` and a `recv()` method.

The following code shows a simple usage for the pipe construct, similar to the preceding Queue example. This script will create two processes: one that will generate random numbers and send them through the pipe and one that will read the same one and write the numbers to a file:

```
from multiprocessing import Pipe, Process
import random

def generate(pipe):
    while True:
      value = random.randrange(10)
      pipe.send(value)
      print "Value sent: %s" % (value)

def reader(pipe):
    f = open("output.txt", "w")
    while True:
      value = pipe.recv()
      f.write(str(value))
      print "."


input_p, output_p = Pipe()
```

```
p1 = Process(target=generate, args=(input_p,))
p2 = Process(target=reader, args=(output_p,))

p1.start()
p2.start()
```

Events

They are also present in the multiprocessing module, and they work in almost a similar way. The developer only needs to keep in mind that event objects can't be passed into worker functions. If you try to do that, a runtime error will be issued, saying that semaphore objects can only be shared between processes through inheritance. This means that you can't do what is shown in this code:

```
from multiprocessing import Process, Event, Pool
import time

event = Event()
event.set()

def worker(i, e):
    if e.is_set():
      time.sleep(0.1)
      print "A - %s" % (time.time())
      e.clear()
    else:
      time.sleep(0.1)
      print "B - %s" % (time.time())
      e.set()

pool = Pool(3)
pool.map(worker, [ (x, event) for x in range(9)])
Instead, you'd have to do something like this:
from multiprocessing import Process, Event, Pool
import time

event = Event()
event.set()

def worker(i):
    if event.is_set():
      time.sleep(0.1)
      print "A - %s" % (time.time())
      event.clear()
    else:
```

```
        time.sleep(0.1)
        print "B - %s" % (time.time())
        event.set()

pool = Pool(3)
pool.map(worker, range(9))
```

Summary

Now that we've covered both alternatives, their main characteristics, and their ups and downs, it is really up to the developer to pick one or the other. There is clearly no better one, since they are meant for different scenarios, although they might seem to accomplish the same thing.

The main take-away from this chapter should be the points mentioned earlier, the main characteristics of each approach, and when each one should be used.

In the next chapter, we'll continue with the optimization tools. This time, we will look at Cython (an alternative that allows you to compile your Python code on C) and PyPy (an alternative interpreter written in Python that is not bound to the GIL like CPython is).

6
Generic Optimization Options

In the never-ending road to mastering optimization, we started by covering some tips and tricks in *Chapter 4, Optimize Everything*. In *Chapter 5, Multithreading versus Multiprocessing*, we went over two major optimization strategies: multithreading and multiprocessing. We saw how they help us and when to use them.

Finally, we will deal with one of the many implementations of the Python language (CPython). This implies that there are other alternatives to CPython. In this chapter, we'll cover two of them:

- We'll cover PyPy, an alternative to the standard Python interpreter we've been using throughout the book. This one is written in Python and has some benefits over the standard version.
- We will talk about Cython, an optimizing static compiler, which will allow us to write Python code and tap into the power of C and C++ easily.

Both alternatives will provide developers with the opportunity to run code in a more optimized fashion, depending, of course, on the characteristics of that code. For each option, we'll look into what exactly they are, how to install them, and some example code on how to use them.

PyPy

Just like CPython is the standard implementation of the Python specifications and is written in C (of course), PyPy is an alternative implementation of Python, both for version 2.x and 3.x. It tries to mimic the behavior of the language that is written in RPython, a limited version of Python with static types.

The PyPy project (http://pypy.org/) is a continuation of another, older project called Psycho, which was a JIT compiler for Python, written in C. It worked great on 32-bit Intel processors, but it was never updated. Its latest stable release was in 2007, so it is now deprecated. PyPy took over in 2007 with its 1.0 release. Although it was initially considered a research project, it grew over the years. Finally, in 2010, version 1.4 was released. With this version, there was an increase in confidence that systems written in PyPy were production ready and compatible with Python 2.5.

The latest stable version of PyPy, released in June 2014, is version 2.5, which, in turn, is compatible with Python 2.7. There is also a beta release of PyPy3, which is, as expected, a version of PyPy that is compatible with Python 3.x.

The reason we will go over PyPy as a viable way of optimization for our scripts is due to these features:

- **Speed**: One of the main features of PyPy is its speed boost over regular Python. This is due to the in-built **Just-in-time** (**JIT**) compiler. It provides flexibility over statically compiled code, since it can adapt to the current platform (processor type, OS version, and so on) during execution time. On the other hand, a statically compiled program would need one executable or every single combination of cases.

- **Memory**: Memory-consuming scripts will consume much less memory when executed using PyPy than with regular CPython.

- **Sandboxing**: PyPy provides a sandboxing environment where every call to an external C library is stubbed. These calls communicate with an external process that handles the actual policy. Although this feature is promising, it is still only a prototype and needs more work to become useful.

- **Stackless**: PyPy also provides a somewhat equivalent set of language features to the ones provided by Stackless Python (http://www.stackless.com/). Some may even consider it a more powerful and flexible version than the latter.

Installing PyPy

There are several ways to install PyPy into your system:

- You can download the binary files directly from their page (http://pypy. org/download.html#default-with-a-jit-compiler). Just make sure you download the right file, according to the OS indication next to the link on their website. Otherwise, there is a good chance it won't work on your system:

---

may have more luck trying out Squeaky's portable Linux binaries.

Python2.7 compatible PyPy 2.5.1

Make sure you have the right OS

- o Linux x86 binary (32bit, tar.bz2 built on Ubuntu 12.04 - 14.04) (see [1] below)

- o Linux x86-64 binary (64bit, tar.bz2 built on Ubuntu 12.04 - 14.04) (see [1] below)

- o ARM Hardfloat Linux binary (ARMHF/gnueabihf, tar.bz2, Raspbian) (see [1] below)

- o ARM Hardfloat Linux binary (ARMHF/gnueabihf, tar.bz2, Ubuntu Raring) (see [1] below)

- o ARM Softfloat Linux binary (ARMEL/gnueabi, tar.bz2, Ubuntu Precise) (see [1] below)

- o Mac OS/X binary (64bit)

- o Windows binary (32bit) (you might need the VS 2008 runtime library installer vcredist_x86.exe.)

- o Source (tar.bz2); Source (zip). See below for more about the sources.

- o All our downloads, including previous versions. We also have a mirror, but please use only if you have troubles accessing the links above

---

If you're using a Linux distribution or OS X, you can check whether its official package repository contains the PyPy package. Normally, systems such as Ubuntu, Debian, Homebrew, MacPorts, Fedora, Gentoo, and Arch tend to have it already. For Ubuntu, you can use the following line of code:

```
$ sudo apt-get install pypy
```

- Finally, another option is to download the source code and compile it yourself. This might be a harder task than downloading the binaries. However, if done correctly, it would assure you that the resulting installation is fully compatible with your system.

Be warned though, compiling from source might sound like an easy task, but it will take a considerable amount of time. On an i7 with 8 GB of RAM, the entire process took about an hour, as shown in the following screenshot:

```
[Timer] Timings:
[Timer] annotate                        ---   383.3 s
[Timer] rtype_lltype                    ---   558.3 s
[Timer] pyjitpl_lltype                  ---   666.0 s
[Timer] backendopt_lltype               ---   172.5 s
[Timer] stackcheckinsertion_lltype      ---   221.3 s
[Timer] database_c                      ---   216.2 s
[Timer] source_c                        ---   275.1 s
[Timer] compile_c                       ---   956.9 s
[Timer] ============================================
[Timer] Total:                          ---  3449.5 s
```

A Just-in-time compiler

This is one of the main features provided by PyPy. It's the main reason for its superior speed results compared to regular Python (CPython).

According to PyPy's official site, the performance might vary depending on the task, but on average, this compiler claims to be seven times faster than CPython.

Normally, with standard compiled programs, we translate the entire source code into machine code before we even execute it the first time. Otherwise, we won't be able to try it. This is the standard set of steps that normally compiled programs go through (preprocessing and translation of the source code, and finally, assembling and linking).

JIT means that the compilation of our code will take place during execution time instead of before it. What normally happens is that the code is translated in a two-step process:

1. First, the original source code is translated into an intermediate language. For some languages, such as Java, it is called bytecode.

2. After we have the bytecode, we start compiling it and translating it into machine code, but only when we need it. One of the peculiarities of JIT compilers is that they only compile the code that needs to be run, and not everything at once.

The second step is what differentiates this type of implementation from other interpreted languages, such as CPython, when the bytecode is interpreted instead of being compiled. Additionally, JIT compilers normally cache compiled code so that the next time it is needed, the overhead of compilation will be avoided.

With all of this in mind, it is clear that for a program to take real advantage of a JIT compiler, it needs to run for at least a few seconds so that the instruction caching can take effect. Otherwise, the effect might be the opposite of what is intended, since the overhead of the compilation will be the only real-time difference that the developer will notice.

One of the main advantages of using a JIT compiler is that the program being executed is able to optimize the machine code for the specific system it is running on (including CPU, OS, and so on). Thus, it provides a level of flexibility that is completely out of scope for static compiled (and even interpreted) programs.

Sandboxing

Although the sandboxing feature of PyPy is still considered as a prototype, we'll cover its basics internal workings to understand the potential it provides.

Sandboxing consists of providing a safe environment where untrusted Python code can run without any fear of causing harm to the host system.

This is achieved in PyPy in particular through a two-process model:

1. On one side, we have a customized version of PyPy compiled specifically to function in the sandbox mode. In particular, this means that any library or system call (I/O for instance) gets marshaled into `stdout` waiting for a marshaled response back.

2. On the other hand, we have a container process, which could be running using PyPy or CPython. This process will take care of answering the library and system calls from the internal PyPy process:

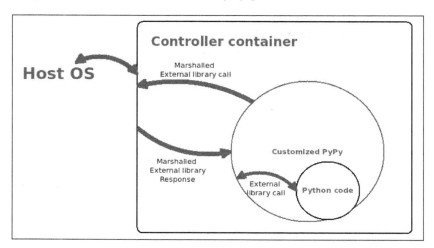

The preceding diagram shows the entire process where a piece of Python code that is executed in the sandbox mode is doing an external library call.

The container process is the one that decides what type of virtualization it provides. For instance, the inner process could be creating file handlers, which, in reality, are being faked by the container process. The process acts as a layer between the real OS and the sandboxed process.

Note that the mechanics explained earlier are very different from sandboxing at the language level. The entire set of instructions is available to the developer. Thus, you achieve a very transparent and secure system with code that could very well run on a standard system and on a secured one.

Optimizing for the JIT

Like we already discussed, the JIT from PyPy is what sets it apart from CPython's implementation. It is this same feature that makes it so fast when running Python code.

Just using PyPy directly on our unchanged Python code, we'll most likely get better results. However, we should take into account some guidelines if we want to optimize our code even further.

Think of functions

JIT works by analyzing which functions are "hotter" (get executed more times) than others. Thus, we're better off structuring our code into functions, specifically for functions that will be executed repeatedly.

Let's see a quick example. The following code will show the time difference between doing the same calculation directly inline versus having it encapsulated inside a function and dealing with the added time relating to the function lookup and the function call itself:

```python
import math
import time

TIMES = 10000000

init = time.clock()
for i in range(TIMES):
    value = math.sqrt(i * math.fabs(math.sin(i - math.cos(i))))

print "No function: %s" % ( init - time.clock())

def calcMath(i):
```

```
        return math.sqrt(i * math.fabs(math.sin(i - math.cos(i))))
init = time.clock()
for i in range(TIMES):
    value = calcMath(i)
print "Function: %s" % ( init - time.clock())
```

The code is very simple, but you can still see how the second output shows that it is the faster implementation. Regular old CPython will work the opposite way, since there is no real-time optimization of the code. The second approach will yield slightly worse results because of the overhead of the function lookup and function call code. However, PyPy and its JIT prove once again that if you want to optimize your code for them, you need to stop thinking the old way.

```
fernando@dune:~/workspace/writing/python/chapter6$ pypy pypy_jit_test.py
No function: -0.910388
Function: -0.909176                    JIT's optimized code
fernando@dune:~/workspace/writing/python/chapter6$ python pypy_jit_test.py
No function: -4.332882
Function: -4.899006                    CPython's standard run
```

The results from the preceding screenshot show what we've been discussing so far:

- PyPy runs the same code considerably faster than CPython
- The JIT is optimizing our code in real time while CPython isn't

Consider using cStringIO to concatenate strings

This is not a small optimization, with respect to both code changes and achieved optimization. We've already covered the fact that for Python, strings are immutable objects. So, if we want to concatenate a large number of strings into a single one, we would be better off doing it with another structure instead of the string itself, since that would yield the worst performance.

In the case of PyPy, it still holds true. However, instead of using lists as the best option, we'll use the cStringIO module (http://pymotw.com/2/StringIO/), which, as we'll see, provides the best results.

Note that because of the nature of PyPy, mentioning cStringIO instead of StringIO might be confusing, since we're referencing a C standard library instead of a pure Python one. This is correct and valid, since some of the C standard libraries common to CPython also work correctly on PyPy. In our case, the following code will calculate the time needed to perform the same concatenation operation in three different ways (using simple strings, using the cStringIO library, and finally, using lists):

```python
from cStringIO import StringIO
import time

TIMES = 100000

init = time.clock()
value = ''
for i in range(TIMES):
    value += str(i)
print "Concatenation: %s" % ( init - time.clock())

init = time.clock()
value = StringIO()
for i in range(TIMES):
    value.write(str(i))
print "StringIO: %s" % ( init - time.clock())

init = time.clock()
value = []
for i in range(TIMES):
    value.append(str(i))
finalValue = ''.join(value)
print "List: %s" % ( init - time.clock())
```

Out of the three alternatives, StringIO is the best one in PyPy. It is much better than simple string concatenation, and even slightly better than using lists.

If we run the same code through CPython, we will get different results. Thus, the best solution is still using lists.

```
fernando@dune:~/workspace/writing/python/chapter6$ pypy pypy_str_vs_stringio.py
Concatenation: -5.557533
StringIO: -0.005191            PyPy is optimizing the StringIO version better
List: -0.009325
fernando@dune:~/workspace/writing/python/chapter6$ python pypy_str_vs_stringio.py
Concatenation: -0.028069
StringIO: -0.031069            CPython on the other hand, optimizes the List approach
List: -0.021833
```

The preceding screenshot corroborates this. Note how with PyPy, the first approach is especially bad performance-wise.

Actions that disable the JIT

Although not directly an optimization, there are some specific methods that will disable the effectiveness of the JIT if we use them. So, it's important to know about these methods.

The following three methods from the `sys` module disable the JIT (according to the current version of PyPy; this could, of course, change in the future):

- `_getframe`: This method returns a frame object from the `callstack`. It even accepts an optional depth parameter that returns frame objects back from the `callstack`. The performance penalty is quite big, so its use is recommended only when it is absolutely needed, such as when developing a debugger.

- `exc_info`: This method returns a tuple of three elements that provide information about the exception being handled. These elements are `type`, `value`, and `traceback`. They are explained here:
    - `type`: This is the type of the exception being handled
    - `value`: This gets the exception parameter
    - `traceback`: This gets the `traceback` object, which encapsulates a `callstack` object the moment the exception was thrown

- `settrace`: This method sets the tracing function, which allows you to trace Python code from within Python. As mentioned earlier, its use is not recommended unless it is absolutely necessary, since it needs to disable the JIT in order to work properly.

Code sample

As a final example for this topic, let's take a look at the code from the `great_circle` function (explained later). The great circle calculation consists of finding the distance between two points on the earth's surface.

The script will do a `for` loop of 5 million iterations. In particular, it calls the same function over and over (5 million times to be precise). This scenario is less than ideal for the CPython interpreter, since it will complete the function lookup that many times.

However, on the other hand and as we've already mentioned, calling the same function over time allows for PyPy's JIT to start optimizing that call. This basically means that in our case, the code is already somewhat optimized for PyPy:

```
import math

def great_circle(lon1,lat1,lon2,lat2):
    radius = 3956 #miles
    x = math.pi/180.0

    a = (90.0-lat1)*(x)
    b = (90.0-lat2)*(x)
    theta = (lon2-lon1)*(x)
    c = math.acos((math.cos(a)*math.cos(b)) +
    (math.sin(a)*math.sin(b)*math.cos(theta)))
    return radius*c


lon1, lat1, lon2, lat2 = -72.345, 34.323, -61.823, 54.826
num = 5000000

for i in range(num):great_circle(lon1,lat1,lon2,lat2)
```

The preceding code can be further optimized following the same principle we just mentioned. We can remove one line from the `great_circle` function into a separate function, optimizing that execution even further, as shown here:

```
import math

def calcualte_acos(a, b ,theta):
  return math.acos((math.cos(a)*math.cos(b)) +
  (math.sin(a)*math.sin(b)*math.cos(theta)))

def great_circle(lon1,lat1,lon2,lat2):
    radius = 3956 #miles
```

```
x = math.pi/180.0

a = (90.0-lat1)*(x)
b = (90.0-lat2)*(x)
theta = (lon2-lon1)*(x)
c = calcualte_acos(a, b, theta)
return radius*c


lon1, lat1, lon2, lat2 = -72.345, 34.323, -61.823, 54.826
num = 5000000

for i in range(num):
  great_circle(lon1,lat1,lon2,lat2)
```

You can see how we moved the `acos` calculation into a separate function, since it was the most expensive line in the entire function (there is a total of six trig functions being called there). By moving that line into another function, we allowed the JIT to take care of optimizing its calls.

In the end, due to that simple change and the fact that we're using PyPy instead of regular Python, we have an execution time of 0.5 seconds. If, on the other hand, we were to run that same code using regular CPython, we would get a time of 4.5 seconds (on my current machine), which is considerably slower.

Cython

Although technically, Cython (`http://cython.org/`) is not exactly an alternative to using the standard CPython interpreter, it will let us write Python code and compile it into C (something CPython doesn't do).

You'll see that Cython could be considered a transpiler, which simply means it's a piece of software meant to translate source code from one language into another. There are other similar products out there, such as CoffeeScript and Dart. Both are very different languages, and both are translated into JavaScript.

In our case, Cython translates a super set of Python (an extended version of the language) into optimized C/C++ code. Then, it's compiled into a Python extension module. This, in turn, allows the developer to:

- Write Python code that calls back and forth C or C++ code natively
- Tune Python code into C-level performance using static-type declarations

Static typing is the key feature that allows this transpiler to generate optimized C code, thus letting Cython move out of the dynamic nature of Python into a more static, yet faster, territory (sometimes, even by several orders of magnitude).

This, of course, makes the Python code more verbose, which, in turn, might hurt other aspects such as maintainability and readability. So, normally, using static typing is not recommended unless there is some kind of proof that clearly shows that adding it will indeed generate a faster running code.

All C types are available for developers to use. Cython is prepared to automatically perform type conversion on assignment. In the special case of Python's arbitrary long integers, when casting to C's integers, a Python overflow error will be raised if an overflow does happen.

The following table shows the same example written in pure Python and the Cython version:

Python version	Cython version
```def f(x): return x**2-x def integrate_f(a, b, N): s = 0 dx = (b-a)/N for i in range(N): s += f(a+i*dx) return s * dx```	```def f(double x): return x**2-x def integrate_f(double a, double b, int N): cdef int i cdef double s, dx s = 0 dx = (b-a)/N for i in range(N): s += f(a+i*dx) return s * dx```

The main difference in both codes is highlighted. It is only the definition of the types of every variable, both the parameters received by both functions, and the local variables used. With this alone, Cython can generate an optimized C version of the code on the left-hand side.

Installing Cython

There are a couple of ways to install Cython into your system. However, for every case, the common requirement is to have a C compiler previously installed. We will not go over the steps required for this, because the instructions might vary from system to system.

Once the C compiler is installed, in order to get Cython, you can perform these steps:

1. Download the latest release from their website (`http://cython.org`), unpack the tarball file, enter the directory, and run the following command:

   `$python setup.py install`

2. If you have the setup tools installed in your system, you can run this command:

   `$pip install cython`

> If you're already using one of the following development environments, it's quite likely that Cython is already installed in your system. However, you can use the earlier steps to update your current version as well:
> - Anaconda
> - Enthought Canopy
> - PythonXY
> - Sage

Building a Cython module

Cython is able to compile our code into C modules, which we can later import into our main code. In order to do this, you need to carry out the following steps:

1. First, a `.pyx` file needs to be compiled (or translated) into a `.c` file by Cython. These are the source code files, basically Python code with some extensions added by Cython. We'll see some examples in a bit.

2. The `.c` file will, in turn, be compiled into a `.so` library by the C compiler. This library can later be imported by Python.

3. There are several ways in which we can compile the code, as explained earlier:

   ° We can create a `distutils` setup file. Distutils is a module that facilitates the creation of other modules, so we can use it to generate our custom C-compiled ones.

   ° We can run the `cython` command line to create a `.c` file from the `.pyx` one. Then, use the C compiler to manually compile the C code into the library.

   ° Finally, another option would be to use the `pyximport` module and import the `.pyx` files as if they were `.py` files.

4. To illustrate the preceding points, let's look at an example using the `distutils` option:

```
#test.pyx
def join_n_print(parts):
    print ' '.join(parts)
```

```
#test.py
from test import join_n_print
join_n_print( ["This", "is", "a", "test"] )
```

```
#setup.py
from distutils.core import setup
from Cython.Build import cythonize

setup(
  name = 'Test app',
  ext_modules = cythonize("test.pyx"),
)
```

5. That's it! The preceding code that is to be exported should be inside the `.pyx` file. The `setup.py` file will normally be the same. It will call the `setup` function with different variations of the parameters. Finally, it will call the `test.py` file, which imports our compiled library and makes use of it.

6. To effectively compile the code, you can use the following command:

```
$ python setup.py build_ext -inplace
```

The following screenshot shows the output from the preceding command. You can see how it doesn't just translate (cythonize) the code, but also compiles the library using the C compiler installed:

```
Compiling test.pyx because it changed.
Cythonizing test.pyx
running build_ext
building 'test' extension
x86_64-linux-gnu-gcc -pthread -fno-strict-aliasing -DNDEBUG -g -fwrapv -O2 -Wall -Wstrict-prototypes
.7/test.o
x86_64-linux-gnu-gcc -pthread -shared -Wl,-O1 -Wl,-Bsymbolic-functions -Wl,-Bsymbolic-functions -Wl,-
rototypes -D_FORTIFY_SOURCE=2 -g -fstack-protector --param=ssp-buffer-size=4 -Wformat -Werror=format-
orkspace/writing/python/chapter6/test.so
```

The preceding example shows a very simple module. However, normally, for more complex cases, a Cython module is comprised of two types of files:

- **Definition files**: These have a .pxd extension and contain C declarations of names that need to be available to other Cython modules.
- **Implementation files**: These have a .pyx extension and contain the actual implementation of the functions declared on the .pxd files.

Definition files normally contain C type declarations, external C functions or variable declarations, and declarations of C functions defined in the module. They cannot contain the implementation of any C or Python function, nor can they contain the definition of any Python class or any executable lines.

On the other hand, an implementation file can have almost any kind of Cython statement.

Here is a typical two-file module example taken from Cython's official documentation (http://docs.cython.org/src/userguide/sharing_declarations.html); it shows how to import .pxd files:

```
#dishes.pxd
cdef enum otherstuff:
    sausage, eggs, lettuce

cdef struct spamdish:
    int oz_of_spam
    otherstuff filler


#restaurant.pyx:
cimport dishes
from dishes cimport spamdish

cdef void prepare(spamdish *d):
    d.oz_of_spam = 42
    d.filler = dishes.sausage

def serve():
    cdef spamdish d
    prepare(&d)
    print "%d oz spam, filler no. %d" % (d.oz_of_spam, d.filler)
```

By default, when cimport is executed, it will look for a file called modulename.pxd in the search path. Whenever the definition file changes, each file importing it will need to be recompiled. Luckily, for us, the Cythin.Build.cythonize utility will take care of that.

Calling C functions

Just like regular Python, Cython allows the developer to directly interface with C by calling functions compiled in external libraries. To import these libraries, the procedure is similar to the standard Python procedure:

```
from libc.stdlib cimport atoi
```

The `cimport` statement is used in implementation or definition files in order to gain access to names declared in other files. Its syntax is exactly the same as standard Python's `import` statement.

If you also need to access the definition of some types defined in a library, you would need the header file (`.h` file). For these cases, with Cython it is not as simple as referencing the file. You'll also need to redeclare the types and structures you will use:

```
cdef extern from "library.h":
  int library_counter;
  char *pointerVar;
```

The preceding example performs the following actions for Cython:

- It lets Cython know how to place a `#include` statement in the generated C code, referencing the library we're including
- It prevents Cython from generating any C code for the declarations inside the block
- It treats all declarations inside the block as if they were made with `cdef extern`, which, in turn, means those declarations are defined elsewhere

Note that this syntax is required because Cython does not, at any moment, read the content of the header file. So, you still need to redeclare the content for it. As a caveat, you technically only need to redeclare the part that you'll use, leaving out anything that's not directly needed by your code. For instance, if you had a big structure declared in your header file with a lot of members, you could redeclare it with only the members you'd need. This would work since during compiling time, the C compiler would use the original code with the full version of the structure.

Solving naming conflicts

An interesting problem arises when names from the imported functions are the same as the ones from your functions.

Say, you have your `myHeader.h` file that defines the `print_with_colors` function, and you need to wrap it in some Python function that you also want to call `print_with_colors`; Cython provides a way for you to work around this and keep the names as you want them.

You can add `extern` C function declarations into a Cython declaration file (`.pxd` file) and then `cimport` it into your Cython code file as follows:

```
#my_declaration.pxd
cdef extern "myHeader.h":
  void print_with_colors(char *)
```

```
#my_cython_code.pyx
from my_declaration cimport print_with_colors as c_print_with_colors

def print_with_colors(str):
  c_print_with_colors(str)
```

You can also avoid renaming the function and use the name of the declaration file as a prefix:

```
#my_cython_code.pyx
cimport  my_declaration
def print_with_colors(str):
  my_declaration.print_with_colors(str)
```

 Both alternatives are valid, and the decision of using one over the other is completely up to the developer. For more information on this subject, head to: `http://docs.cython.org/src/userguide/external_C_code.html`.

Defining types

As mentioned earlier, Cython allows the developer to define the type of a variable or the return type of a function. In both cases, the keyword used for this is `cdef`. Typing is actually optional, since Cython will try to optimize the Python code by turning it into C. That being said, defining the static types where they're needed will certainly help.

Let's now look at a very basic example of a piece of code in Python and how the same code executes in its three versions: pure Python, compiled by Cython without typing, and finally, compiled and using typing.

The code is as follows:

Python	Cython
| ```
def is_prime(num):
    for j in range(2,num):
        if (num % j) == 0:
            return False
    return True
``` | ```
def is_prime(int num):
    cdef int j;
    for j in range(2,num):
        if (num % j) == 0:
            return False
    return True
``` |

Thanks to the fact that we're declaring the `for` loop variable as a C integer. Cython will turn this loop into an optimized C `for` loop, which will be one of the major improvements to this code.

Now, we will set up a main file that will import that function:

```
import sys
from <right-module-name> import is_prime


def main(argv):

    if (len(sys.argv) != 3):
        sys.exit('Usage: prime_numbers.py <lowest_bound> <upper_bound>')

    low = int(sys.argv[1])
    high = int(sys.argv[2])

    for i in range(low,high):
        if is_prime(i):
            print i,

if __name__ == "__main__":
    main(sys.argv[1:])
```

Then, we will execute our script like this:

```
$ time python script.py 10 10000
```

We will get the following interesting results:

Pure Python version	Compiled without typing	Compiled with typing
0.792 seconds	0.694 seconds	0.043 seconds

Even though the non-optimized version of the code is faster than the pure Python one, we only see the real power of Cython when we start declaring the types.

Defining types during function definitions

There are two different types of functions that can be defined in Cython:

- **Standard Python functions**: These are normal functions that are exactly like the ones declared in pure Python code. To do this, you need the standard cdef keyword, and these functions will receive Python objects as parameters and also return Python objects.

- **C functions**: These are the optimized versions of the standard functions. They take either Python objects or C values as parameters and can also return both. To define these, you need the special cdef keyword.

Either type of function can be called from within a Cython module. However (and this is a very important difference), if you want to call your functions from within your Python code, you either need to make sure the function is declared as standard or you need to use the special cpdef keyword. This keyword will create a wrapper object for the function. So, when the function is called from within Cython, it'll use the C function, and when called from within Python code, it'll use the Python version.

When dealing with C types for the parameters of the function, an automatic conversion will be done (if possible) from the Python object to the C value. This is only currently possible for numeric types, strings, and struct types. If you attempt to use any other type, it will result in a compile-time error.

The following simple example illustrates the difference between both modes:

```
#my_functions.pxd

#this is a pure Python function, so Cython will create a make it
return and receive Python objects instead of primitive types.
cdef full_python_function (x):
```

```
        return x**2

#This function instead, is defined as both, a standard function and an
optimized C function, thanks to the use of the cpdef keyword.
cpdef int c_function(int num):
        return x**2
```

 If the return type or the type of parameter is left undefined, then it will be assumed to be a Python object.

Finally, C functions that don't return a Python object have no way to report Python exceptions to its caller. So, when an error occurs, a warning message is printed and the exception is ignored. This is, of course, far from ideal. Luckily, for us, there is a way around this.

We can use the except keyword during function definition. This keyword specifies that whenever an exception occurs inside the function, a specific value will be returned. Here is an example:

```
cdef int text(double param) except -1:
```

With the preceding code, whenever an exception occurs, -1 will be returned. It is important that you don't manually return the exception value from your function. This is especially relevant if you define False to be your exception value because any False value will do here.

For cases where any possible return value is a valid return value, then there is an alternate notation that you can use:

```
cdef int text(double param) except? -1:
```

The ? sign sets -1 as a possible exception value. When returned, Cython will call PyErr_Occurred() to make sure that it is really an error and not just a normal return action.

There is one more variation of the except keyword, which makes sure to call PyErr_Occurred() after every return:

```
cdef int text(double param) except *:
```

The only real use of the preceding notation is for functions returning void that need to propagate errors. This is because in these special cases, there is no value to check; otherwise, there is no real use case for it.

A Cython example

Let's take a quick look at the same example we used for PyPy. It shows us how to improve the performance of a script. The code will again do the same calculation 5 million times: from math, import PI, acos, cos, and sin:

```
def great_circle(lon1,lat1,lon2,lat2):
    radius = 3956 #miles
    x = PI/180.0

    a = (90.0-lat1)*(x)
    b = (90.0-lat2)*(x)
    theta = (lon2-lon1)*(x)
    c = acos((cos(a)*cos(b)) +

                    (sin(a)*sin(b)*cos(theta)))
    return radius*c
```

Then, we will test it by running the function 5,000,000 times with the following script:

```
from great_circle_py import great_circle

lon1, lat1, lon2, lat2 = -72.345, 34.323, -61.823, 54.826
num = 5000000

for i in range(num):
  great_circle(lon1,lat1,lon2,lat2)
```

Again, as I've already mentioned earlier, if we run this script using the time command-line utility from Linux with the CPython interpreter, we will see that the resulting execution takes around 4.5 seconds to run (in my current system). Your numbers will most likely be different.

Instead of going to the profiler, like we did in earlier chapters, we'll go directly to Cython now. We'll implement some of the improvements we've been discussing into a Cython module that we can import from our test script.

Here's our first try at it:

```
#great_circle_cy_v1.pyx
from math import pi as PI, acos, cos, sin

def great_circle(double lon1,double lat1,double lon2,double lat2):
```

```
        cdef double a, b, theta, c, x, radius


        radius = 3956 #miles
        x = PI/180.0

        a = (90.0-lat1)*(x)
        b = (90.0-lat2)*(x)
        theta = (lon2-lon1)*(x)
        c = acos((cos(a)*cos(b)) +
                    (sin(a)*sin(b)*cos(theta)))
        return radius*c
#great_circle_setup_v1.py
from distutils.core import setup
from Cython.Build import cythonize

setup(
   name = 'Great Circle module v1',
   ext_modules = cythonize("great_circle_cy_v1.pyx"),
)
```

As you can see in the preceding code, all we did was give a C type to all the variables and parameters we're using in our code. This alone took the execution time from 4.5 seconds down to 3. We shaved off 1.5 seconds, but we can probably do better.

Our code is still using a Python library `math`. Since Cython allows us to mix Python and C libraries, it comes in handy when we're in a hurry. It takes care of the conversions for us, but as we can see here, not without a cost. Let's now try to remove the dependency of that Python library and call upon C's `math.h` file:

```
#great_circle_cy_v2.pyx
cdef extern from "math.h":
    float cosf(float theta)
    float sinf(float theta)
    float acosf(float theta)

def great_circle(double lon1,double lat1,double lon2,double lat2):
    cdef double a, b, theta, c, x, radius
    cdef double pi = 3.141592653589793

    radius = 3956 #miles
    x = pi/180.0

    a = (90.0-lat1)*(x)
```

```
b = (90.0-lat2)*(x)
theta = (lon2-lon1)*(x)
c = acosf((cosf(a)*cosf(b)) +
          (sinf(a)*sinf(b)*cosf(theta)))
return radius*c
```

After removing all references to the math Python library and working directly with C's math.h file, we went from the 3.5 seconds in our previously optimized code to an amazing 0.95 seconds.

When to define a type

The previous example might seem obvious and simple to optimize. However, for bigger scripts, redeclaring every variable as a C variable and importing all C libraries instead of Python ones (whenever possible) is not always the best way to go.

Going about it this way will lead to readability and maintainability issues. It will also hurt the inherent flexibility of Python code. It could, in fact, even end up hurting the performance by adding unnecessary type checks and conversions. So, there must be a way to determine the best places to add types and switch libraries. This way is using Cython. Cython comes with the ability to annotate your source code and show you, very graphically, how each line of code can be translated into C code.

Using the -a attribute in Cython, you can generate an HTML file that will highlight your code with yellow. The more yellow a line is, the more C-API interactions are required to translate that piece of code into C. White lines (lines without any color) are directly translated into C. Let's look at how our original code is rendered under this new tool:

```
$ cython -a great_circle_py.py
```

The following screenshot shows the HTML file generated from the preceding command:

```
Generated by Cython 0.22

Raw output: great circle py.c

+01: import math
 02:
+03: def great_circle(lon1,lat1,lon2,lat2):
+04:     radius = 3956 #miles
+05:     x = math.pi/180.0
 06:
+07:     a = (90.0-lat1)*(x)
+08:     b = (90.0-lat2)*(x)
+09:     theta = (lon2-lon1)*(x)
+10:     c = math.acos((math.cos(a)*math.cos(b)) +
+11:             (math.sin(a)*math.sin(b)*math.cos(theta)))
+12:     return radius*c
```

We can clearly see that most of our code needs at least a few interactions with the C-API in order to be translated into C (only line 4 is completely white). It is important to understand that our aim should be to get as many lines to white as possible. The lines with a + sign indicate that they can be clicked, and the C code generated will be displayed, as shown here:

```
Generated by Cython 0.22

Raw output: great circle py.c

+01: import math
 02:
+03: def great_circle(lon1,lat1,lon2,lat2):
+04:     radius = 3956 #miles
+05:     x = math.pi/180.0
    __pyx_t_1 = __Pyx_GetModuleGlobalName(__pyx_n_s_math); if (unlikely(!__pyx_t_1
    __Pyx_GOTREF(__pyx_t_1);
    __pyx_t_2 = __Pyx_PyObject_GetAttrStr(__pyx_t_1, __pyx_n_s_pi); if (unlikely(!
    __Pyx_GOTREF(__pyx_t_2);
    __Pyx_DECREF(__pyx_t_1); __pyx_t_1 = 0;
    __pyx_t_1 = __Pyx_PyNumber_Divide(__pyx_t_2, __pyx_float_180_0); if (unlikely(
    __Pyx_GOTREF(__pyx_t_1);
    __Pyx_DECREF(__pyx_t_2); __pyx_t_2 = 0;
    __pyx_v_x = __pyx_t_1;
    __pyx_t_1 = 0;
 06:
+07:     a = (90.0-lat1)*(x)
+08:     b = (90.0-lat2)*(x)
+09:     theta = (lon2-lon1)*(x)
+10:     c = math.acos((math.cos(a)*math.cos(b)) +
+11:             (math.sin(a)*math.sin(b)*math.cos(theta)))
+12:     return radius*c
```

Now, by looking at our results, we can see that the lighter yellow lines are the simple assignments (lines 5, 7, 8, and 9). They can be easily fixed by doing what we initially did: declare those variables as C variables instead of letting them be Python objects, which would require us to convert code.

By doing the conversion, we will get something like the next screenshot. This screenshot shows the resulting report from analyzing the great_circle_cy_v1.pyx file:

```
Generated by Cython 0.22

Raw output: great circle cy v1.c

+01: import math
 02:
+03: def great_circle(double lon1,double lat1,double lon2,double lat2):
 04:     cdef double a, b, theta, c, x, radius
 05:
+06:     radius = 3956 #miles
+07:     x = math.pi/180.0
 08:
+09:     a = (90.0-lat1)*(x)
+10:     b = (90.0-lat2)*(x)
+11:     theta = (lon2-lon1)*(x)
+12:     c = math.acos((math.cos(a)*math.cos(b)) +
+13:                   (math.sin(a)*math.sin(b)*math.cos(theta)))
+14:     return radius*c
```

Much better! Now, those lines are fully white, except line 7, which is still light yellow. This is, of course, because that line is actually referencing the math.pi object. We could fix it simply by initializing the pi variable with a fixed value of PI. However, we still have the big yellow block, that is, lines 12 and 13. This is also due to our usage of the math library. So, after we get rid of it, we will get the following file:

```
Generated by Cython 0.22

Raw output: great circle cy v2.c

01: cdef extern from "math.h":
02:      float cosf(float theta)
03:      float sinf(float theta)
04:      float acosf(float theta)
05:
+06: def great_circle(double lon1,double lat1,double lon2,double lat2):
07:      cdef double a, b, theta, c, x, radius
+08:      cdef double pi = 3.141592653589793
09:
+10:      radius = 3956 #miles
+11:      x = pi/180.0
12:
+13:      a = (90.0-lat1)*(x)
+14:      b = (90.0-lat2)*(x)
+15:      theta = (lon2-lon1)*(x)
+16:      c = acosf((cosf(a)*cosf(b)) +
17:                     (sinf(a)*sinf(b)*cosf(theta)))
+18:      return radius*c
```

The preceding screenshot shows the final code we presented earlier. Almost all of our code is directly translatable to C, and we got a good performance out of it. Now, we still have two yellow lines: 6 and 18.

We can't do much about line 6 because that function is the Python function we need to execute. If we were to declare it with `cdef`, we would not have access to it. However, again, line 18 is not completely white. This is because `great_circle` is a Python function and the returned value is a Python object, which needs to be wrapped and translated into a C value. If we click on it, we can see the generated code:

```
+16:        c = acosf((cosf(a)*cosf(b)) +
 17:                        (sinf(a)*sinf(b)*cosf(theta)))
+18:        return radius*c
    Pyx_XDECREF(__pyx_r);
    __pyx_t_1 = PyFloat_FromDouble((__pyx_v_radius * __pyx_v_c)); if (
    Pyx_GOTREF(__pyx_t_1);
    __pyx_r = __pyx_t_1;
    __pyx_t_1 = 0;
    goto __pyx_L0;
```

The only way we can fix this is by declaring our function with `cpdef`, which will create a wrapper for it. However, it will also let us declare the return type. So, we're no longer returning a Python object. Instead, we're returning a `double` value, and the resulting code and annotated screenshot is as follows:

```
Generated by Cython 0.22

Raw output: great circle cy v3.c

 01: cdef extern from "math.h":
 02:     float cosf(float theta)
 03:     float sinf(float theta)
 04:     float acosf(float theta)
 05:
+06: cpdef double great_circle(double lon1,double lat1,double lon2,double lat2):
 07:     cdef double a, b, theta, c, x, radius
+08:     cdef double pi = 3.141592653589793
 09:
+10:     radius = 3956 #miles
+11:     x = pi/180.0
 12:
+13:     a = (90.0-lat1)*(x)
+14:     b = (90.0-lat2)*(x)
+15:     theta = (lon2-lon1)*(x)
+16:     c = acosf((cosf(a)*cosf(b)) +
 17:                     (sinf(a)*sinf(b)*cosf(theta)))
+18:     return radius*c
    __pyx_r = (__pyx_v_radius * __pyx_v_c);
    goto __pyx_L0;
```

We can see how the C code generated for the returned statement got simplified with this latest change. The performance got a small boost as well, since we went from 0.95 seconds down to 0.8 seconds.

Thanks to our analysis of the code, we were able to go one step further and optimize it a bit more. This technique is a good way to check your progress when optimizing code for Cython. This technique provides a visual and simple indicator of the complexity of the optimized code.

 Note that in this particular case, the results obtained from going the Cython route for this optimization are not as good as the ones obtained using PyPy earlier in this chapter (0.8 seconds with Cython versus 0.5 seconds with PyPy).

Limitations

Everything we've seen so far seems to indicate that Cython is a perfectly viable option to our performance needs. However, the truth is that Cython is not yet 100 percent compatible with the Python syntax. Sadly, there are some limitations that we need to take into consideration before deciding to use this tool for our performance enhancement needs. From the current list of public bugs on the project, we can gather the list of current limitations.

Generator expressions

These expressions are currently the ones that suffer the most, since they have several issues in the current version of Cython. These issues are as follows:

- Using iterables inside the generator expression causes a problem since there are issues with the evaluation scope.
- Also, related to iterables inside a generator, Cython appears to be evaluating them inside the generator's body. On the other hand, CPython does it outside, before creating the actual generator.
- Generators in Cpython have attributes that allow for introspection. Cython is still not fully up to date when it comes to supporting those attributes.

Comparison of char* literals

The current implementation of Cython performs comparsons of byte literals based on the pointers used, instead of the actual value of the string.

```
cdef char* str = "test string"
print str == b"test string"
```

The preceding code will not always print True. It will depend on the pointer used to store the first string instead of depending on the actual string value.

Tuples as function arguments

Although only a Python 2 feature, the language allows for the following syntax:

```
def myFunction( (a,b) ):
    return a + b
args = (1,2)
print myFunction(args)
```

However, the preceding code is not even correctly parsed by Cython. This particular feature is flagged as probably "not fixable" in the future of Cython, since Python 3.x has removed it as well.

 Note that the Cython team is expecting to fix most of the limitations mentioned earlier by the time they release version 1.0.

Stack frames

Currently, Cython is generating fake tracebacks as part of its exception propagation mechanics. They're not filling in locals and co_code values. In order to do this properly, they would have to generate the stack frames on function call time, incurring in a potential performance penalty. So, it is unclear whether they will fix this in the future or not.

How to choose the right option

Up to this point, we've gone over two different alternatives to radically optimize our code. However, how do we know which one is the right one? Or even better, which one is the best one?

The answer to both those questions is the same: *there is no single best or right one.* Whether one of the options is better or worse depends entirely on one or more of these aspects:

- The actual use case you're trying to optimize
- The familiarity of the developer with either Python or C
- The importance of readability of your optimized code
- The amount of time at hand to perform the optimization

When to go with Cython

Here are the situations when you should go with Cython:

- **You're familiar with C code**: It's not like you'll be coding in C, but you will be using principles that are common to C, such as static types, and C libraries, such as `math.h`. So, being familiar with the language and its internals will definitely be helpful.

- **Losing Python's readability is not a problem**: The code you'll write for Cython is not fully Python, so part of its readability will be lost.

- **Full support of the Python language is needed**: Even though Cython is not Python, it is more an extension than a subset of the language. So, if you need full compatibility with the language, Cython might be the right choice.

When to go with PyPy

Here are the situations when you should go with PyPy:

- **You're not dealing with an execute once script**: PyPy's JIT optimization is great if your script is a long running program, with loops that can be optimized, but if instead, the script you're trying to improve will run once and be done, then PyPy is actually slower than the original CPython.

- **Full support of third-party libraries is not required**: Even though PyPy is compatible with Python 2.7.x, it is not fully compatible with its external libraries, especially if they're C libraries. So, depending on your code, PyPy might not really be an option.

- **You need your code to be compatible with CPython**: If you need your code to run for both implementations (PyPy and CPython), then the Cython alternative is completely out of the question. PyPy becomes the only option.

Summary

In this chapter, we have covered two alternatives to the standard Python implementation. One is PyPy, which consists of a version of Python and is implemented in RPython. It has a JIT compiler in charge of optimizing the code during execution time. The other one is Cython, which is basically a transpiler of Python code into C code. We saw how each of them worked, how to install them, and how our code needed to be changed in order to gain benefits from using them.

Finally, we went over a few points on how and when to choose one over the other.

In the next chapter, we'll focus on a very specific use case for Python: number crunching. The topic is very common in the Python community, since the language is very often used for scientific purposes. We'll cover three options that will help us write code faster: Numba, Parakeet, and pandas.

7
Lightning Fast Number Crunching with Numba, Parakeet, and pandas

Number crunching is a topic specific to the programming world. However, given that Python is so often used for scientific research and data science problems, number crunching ends up being a very common topic in the Python world.

That being said, we could just as easily implement our algorithms using the information from the earlier six chapters, and we would most likely end up with pretty fast and performant code. Again, that information is meant to be for generic use cases. There will always be something to say about optimizing for a particular case.

In this chapter, we'll cover three options that will help us write faster and more optimized code focused on scientific problems. For each one, we'll go over the basic installation instructions. We will also look at some code samples showing the benefits of each option.

The tools we'll review in this chapter are as follows:

- **Numba**: This is a module that allows you to write high-performance functions in pure Python by generating optimized machine code.
- **Parakeet**: This is a runtime compiler for scientific operations written in a subset of Python. It is ideal for expressing numerical computations.
- **pandas**: This is a library that provides a set of high-performance data structures and analysis tools.

Numba

Numba (http://numba.pydata.org/) is a module that allows you to indicate (via decorators) to the Python interpreter which functions should be translated into machine code. Numba thus provides equivalent performance to C or Cython without the need to either use a different interpreter or actually code in C.

The module will generate optimized machine code just by requiring it. It can even be compiled to run on either CPU or GPU hardware.

Here is a very basic example taken from their official site, showing how to use it. We'll go into more detail in a bit:

```python
from numba import jit
from numpy import arange

# jit decorator tells Numba to compile this function.
# The argument types will be inferred by Numba when function is
called.
@jit
def sum2d(arr):
    M, N = arr.shape
    result = 0.0
    for i in range(M):
        for j in range(N):
            result += arr[i,j]
    return result

a = arange(9).reshape(3,3)
print(sum2d(a))
```

Note that even though the promise of Numba sounds impressive, the library is meant to optimize operations on arrays. It is considerably tied to NumPy (which we'll review shortly). So, not every function will be optimizable by it, and using it might even hurt performance.

For instance, let's take a look at a similar example, one that doesn't use NumPy and accomplishes a similar task:

```python
from numba import jit
from numpy import arange

# jit decorator tells Numba to compile this function.
# The argument types will be inferred by Numba when function is
called.
@jit
def sum2d(arr):
    M, N = arr.shape
    result = 0.0
    for i in range(M):
        for j in range(N):
            result += arr[i,j]
    return result

a = arange(9).reshape(3,3)
print(sum2d(a))
```

The preceding code has the following execution times, depending on whether we keep the @jit line or not:

- With the @jit line on: 0.3 seconds
- Without the @jit line: 0.1 seconds

Installation

There are actually two ways to install Numba: you can either use the conda package manager from Anaconda, or you can just clone the GitHub repo and compile it.

If you're going for the conda approach, you can install the command-line tool called miniconda (which can be downloaded from http://conda.pydata.org/miniconda.html). After installing it, you can just use the following command:

```
$ conda install numba
```

The following screenshot shows the output from this command. The command lists all packages that will be installed or updated, specifically numpy and llvmlite, which are direct dependencies from Numba:

```
fernando@dune:~$ conda install numba
Fetching package metadata: ....
Solving package specifications: .
Package plan for installation in environment /home/fernando/miniconda:

The following packages will be downloaded:

    package                    |            build
    ---------------------------|-----------------
    enum34-1.0.4               |           py27_0          48 KB
    funcsigs-0.4               |           py27_0          19 KB
    llvmlite-0.4.0             |           py27_0         7.3 MB
    numpy-1.9.2                |           py27_0         7.8 MB
    numba-0.18.2               |       np19py27_1         1.1 MB
    requests-2.7.0             |           py27_0         594 KB
    setuptools-16.0            |           py27_0         341 KB
    conda-3.12.0               |           py27_0         167 KB
    pip-6.1.1                  |           py27_0         1.4 MB
    ------------------------------------------------------------
                                           Total:         18.7 MB

The following NEW packages will be INSTALLED:

    enum34:     1.0.4-py27_0
    funcsigs:   0.4-py27_0
    llvmlite:   0.4.0-py27_0
    numba:      0.18.2-np19py27_1
    numpy:      1.9.2-py27_0
    pip:        6.1.1-py27_0
    setuptools: 16.0-py27_0

The following packages will be UPDATED:

    conda:      3.10.1-py27_0  --> 3.12.0-py27_0
    requests:   2.6.0-py27_0   --> 2.7.0-py27_0

Proceed ([y]/n)? 
```

If, on the other hand, you want to use the source code, you could clone the repo by using this command:

```
$ git clone git://github.com/numba/numba.git
```

You'll need to have numpy and llvmlite installed as well. After that, you can use the following command:

```
$ python setup.py build_ext -inplace
```

Note that the preceding command will succeed even if you don't have the requirements installed. However, you won't be able to use Numba unless you install them.

In order to check whether your installation was successful, you can do a simple check from the Python REPL:

```
>>> import numba
>>> numba.__version__
'0.18.2'
```

Using Numba

Now that you have managed to install Numba, let's take a look at what we can do with it. The main features provided by this module are as follows:

- On-the-fly code generation
- Native code generation for both CPU and GPU hardware
- Integration with Python's scientific software, thanks to the Numpy dependency

Numba's code generation

When it comes to code generation, the main feature of Numba is its @jit decorator. Using it, you can mark a function for optimization under Numba's JIT compiler.

We already talked about the benefits of having a JIT compiler in the previous chapter, so we won't go into the details here. Instead, let's see how to use the decorator for our benefit.

There are several ways to use this decorator. The default one, which is also the recommended way, is the one we already showed earlier:

```
Lazy compilation
```

The following code will cause Numba to generate the optimized code once the function is called. It'll try to infer the types of its attributes and the return type of the function:

```
from numba import jit

@jit
def sum2(a,b):
  return a + b
```

If you call the same function with different types, then different code paths will be generated and optimized.

Eager compilation

On the other hand, if you happen to know the types that your function will receive (and optionally, return), you could pass those to the @jit decorator. Then, only that specific case would be optimized.

The following code shows the added code needed to pass in the function signature:

```
from numba import jit, int32

@jit(int32(int32, int32))
def sum2(a,b):
    return a + b
```

Here are the most common types that are used to specify function signatures:

- void: These are used as the return type for functions not returning anything
- intp and uintp: These are pointer-sized integers, signed and unsigned respectively
- intc and uintc: These are the C equivalent to the int and unsigned int types
- int8, int16, int32, and int64: These are the fix-width integers of the corresponding bit width (for the unsigned version, just add u as a prefix, for instance, uint8)
- float32 and float64: These are single and double-precision floating-point numbers
- complex64 and complex128: These represent single and double-precision complex numbers
- Arrays can also be declared by indexing any of the numeric types, for example, float32[:] for a one-dimensional floating-point number array and int32[:,:] for a two-dimensional integer array

Other configuration settings

Apart from eager compilation, there are two more options we can pass onto the @jit decorator. These options will help us force Numba's optimization. They are described here.

No GIL

Whenever our code is optimized using native types (rather than using Python types), the GIL (which we discussed in *Chapter 6, Generic Optimization Options*) is no longer necessary.

We have a way of disabling the GIL in such cases. We can pass the `nogil=True` attribute to the decorator. This way, we can run Python code (or Numba code) concurrently with other threads.

That being said, remember that if you don't have the GIL limitation, then you will have to deal with the common problems of multithreaded systems (consistency, synchronization, race conditions, and so on).

NoPython mode

This option will let us set the compilation mode of Numba. By default, it will try to jump between modes. It will try to decide the best mode possible depending on the code of the optimized function.

There are two modes that are available. On one hand, there is `object` mode. It generates code capable of handling all Python objects and uses the C API to perform operations on those objects. On the other hand, the `nopython` mode generates much faster code by avoiding the calls to the C API. The only problem with it is that only a subset of functions and methods are available to be used.

The `object` mode will not generate faster code unless Numba can take advantage of loop-jitting (which means that a loop can be extracted and compiled in `nopython` mode).

What we can do is force Numba to go into `nopython` mode and raise an error if such a thing is not possible. This can be done using these lines of code:

```
@jit(nopython=True)
def add2(a, b):
    return a + b
```

The issue with the `nopython` mode is that it has certain restrictions, apart from the limited subset of Python it supports:

- The native types used for all values inside the function have to be capable of being inferred
- No new memory can be allocated inside the function

As an added extra, for loop-jitting to take place, the to-be-optimized loops can't have a return statement inside. Otherwise, they won't be eligible for optimization.

So, let's now look at an example of how this will look for our code:

```python
def sum(x, y):
    array = np.arange(x * y).reshape(x, y)
    sum = 0
    for i in range(x):
        for j in range(y):
            sum += array[i, j]
    return sum
```

The preceding example is taken from the Numba site. It shows a function that is eligible for loop-jitting, also called loop-lifting. To make sure it works as expected, we can use the Python REPL as follows:

```
Python 2.7.9 |Continuum Analytics, Inc.| (default, Apr 14 2015, 12:54:25)
[GCC 4.4.7 20120313 (Red Hat 4.4.7-1)] on linux2
Type "help", "copyright", "credits" or "license" for more information.
Anaconda is brought to you by Continuum Analytics.
Please check out: http://continuum.io/thanks and https://binstar.org
>>> from numba import jit
>>> import numpy as np
>>> @jit
... def sum_auto_jitting(x, y):
...     array = np.arange(x * y).reshape(x, y)
...     sum = 0
...     for i in range(x):
...         for j in range(y):
...             sum += array[i, j]
...     return sum
...
>>>
>>> sum_auto_jitting(2,65)
8385
>>> sum_auto_jitting.inspect_types()
```

Alternatively, we can also call the `inspect_types` method directly from our code. The benefit of the latter is that we'll also have access to the source code of our functions. This is a great advantage when trying to match Numba-generated instructions to lines of code.

The preceding output is useful to understand the behind-the-scenes action that goes on when we optimize our code with Numba. More specifically, we can understand how it infers the types, whether there is any automatic optimization going on, and basically, how many instructions each Python line is translated into.

Let's take a look at the output we would get from calling the `inspect_types` method from within our code (which is considerably more detailed than using the REPL):

 Note that the following code is a reduced version of the entire output. If you want to study it completely, you need to run the command on your computer.

```
sum_auto_jitting (int64, int64)
-----------------------------------------------------------------
-----------
# File: auto-jitting.py
# --- LINE 6 ---

@jit

# --- LINE 7 ---

def sum_auto_jitting(x, y):

    # --- LINE 8 ---
    # label 0
    #   x = arg(0, name=x)    :: pyobject
    #   y = arg(1, name=y)    :: pyobject
    #   $0.1 = global(np: <module 'numpy' from '/home/fernando/
miniconda/lib/python2.7/site-packages/numpy/__init__.pyc'>)   ::
pyobject
    #   $0.2 = getattr(attr=arange, value=$0.1)   :: pyobject
    #   del $0.1
    #   $0.5 = x * y   :: pyobject
    #   $0.6 = call $0.2($0.5, )   :: pyobject
    #   del $0.5
    #   del $0.2
    #   $0.7 = getattr(attr=reshape, value=$0.6)   :: pyobject
    #   del $0.6
    #   $0.10 = call $0.7(x, y, )   :: pyobject
    #   del $0.7
    #   array = $0.10   :: pyobject
    #   del $0.10

    array = np.arange(x * y).reshape(x, y)

    # --- LINE 9 ---
    #   $const0.11 = const(int, 0)   :: pyobject
    #   sum = $const0.11   :: pyobject
```

```
    #    del $const0.11

    sum = 0

    # --- LINE 10 ---
    #    jump 40.1
    # label 40.1
    #    $const40.1.1 = const(LiftedLoop, LiftedLoop(<function
    sum_auto_jitting at 0x7ff5f94756e0>))   :: XXX Lifted Loop XXX
    #    $40.1.6 = call $const40.1.1(y, x, sum, array, )   :: XXX
    Lifted Loop XXX
    #    del y
...

    #    jump 103
    for i in range(x):
        # --- LINE 11 ---
        for j in range(y):
            # --- LINE 12 ---
            sum += array[i, j]
    # --- LINE 13 ---
    # label 103
    #    $103.2 = cast(value=sum.1)   :: pyobject
    #    del sum.1
    #    return $103.2
    return sum
# The function contains lifted loops
# Loop at line 10
# Has 1 overloads
# File: auto-jitting.py
# --- LINE 6 ---

@jit
# --- LINE 7 ---
def sum_auto_jitting(x, y):
    # --- LINE 8 ---
    array = np.arange(x * y).reshape(x, y)
    # --- LINE 9 ---
    sum = 0
    # --- LINE 10 ---
    # label 37
    #    y = arg(0, name=y)   :: int64
    #    x = arg(1, name=x)   :: int64
```

```
#    sum = arg(2, name=sum)   :: int64
#    array = arg(3, name=array)   :: array(int64, 2d, C)
#    $37.1 = global(range: <built-in function range>)   :: range
#    $37.3 = call $37.1(x, )   :: (int64,) -> range_state64
#    del x
#    del $37.1
#    $37.4 = getiter(value=$37.3)   :: range_iter64
#    del $37.3
#    $phi50.1 = $37.4   :: range_iter64
#    del $37.4
#    jump 50
# label 50
#    $50.2 = iternext(value=$phi50.1)   :: pair<int64, bool>
#    $50.3 = pair_first(value=$50.2)   :: int64
#    $50.4 = pair_second(value=$50.2)   :: bool
#    del $50.2
#    $phi53.1 = $50.3   :: int64
#    del $50.3
#    branch $50.4, 53, 102
# label 53
#    i = $phi53.1   :: int64
#    del $phi53.1

for i in range(x):

    # --- LINE 11 ---
    #    jump 56
    # label 56


...


    #    j = $phi72.1   :: int64
    #    del $phi72.1

    for j in range(y):

        # --- LINE 12 ---
        #    $72.6 = build_tuple(items=[Var(i, auto-jitting.py
        (10)), Var(j, auto-jitting.py (11))])   :: (int64 x 2)
        #    del j
        #    $72.7 = getitem(index=$72.6, value=array)   ::
        int64


...
```

```
#    return $103.3

       sum += array[i, j]

# --- LINE 13 ---

return sum
```

In order to understand the preceding output, notice how every commented block starts with the line number of the original source code. It then follows with the instructions generated by that line, and finally, you'll see the uncommented Python line you wrote.

Notice the `LiftedLoop` line. In this line, you can see the automatic optimization done by Numba. Also, notice the type inferred by Numba at the end of most lines. Whenever you see a `pyobject` property, it means that it is not using a native type. Instead, it is using a generic object that wraps all Python types.

Running your code on the GPU

As it's been already mentioned, Numba provides support to run our code on both CPU and GPU hardware. This, in practice, would allow us to improve the performance of certain computations by running them in an environment better suited for parallel computation than the CPU.

More specifically, Numba supports CUDA programming (`http://www.nvidia.com/object/cuda_home_new.html`) by translating a subset of Python functions into CUDA kernels and devices following the CUDA execution model.

CUDA is a parallel computing platform and programming model invented by Nvidia. It enables considerable speed boosts by harnessing the power of GPUs.

GPU programming is a topic that could most likely fill an entire book, so we won't go into details here. Instead, we'll just mention that Numba possesses this capability and that it can be achieved using the `@cuda.jit` decorator. For full documentation on this subject, refer to the official documents at `http://numba.pydata.org/numba-doc/0.18.2/cuda/index.html`.

The pandas tool

The second tool that we'll discuss in this chapter is called pandas (`http://pandas.pydata.org/`). It is an open source library that provides high-performance, easy-to-use data structures, and data-analysis tools for Python.

This tool was invented back in 2008 by developer Wes McKinney while needing a performant solution to perform quantitative analysis on financial data. The library has become one of the most popular and active projects in the Python community.

One thing to note regarding the performance of code written using pandas is that parts of its critical code paths were written using Cython (we covered Cython in *Chapter 6, Generic Optimization Options*).

Installing pandas

Given the popularity of pandas, there are many ways to install it onto your system. It all depends on the type of setup you have.

The recommended way is to directly install the Anaconda Python distribution (`docs.continuum.io/anaconda/`), which comes packed with pandas and the rest of the SciPy stack (such as NumPy, Matplotlib, and so on). This way, by the time you're done, you'd have installed over 100 packages and downloaded several 100 megabytes of data during the process.

If, on the other hand, you don't want to deal with the full Anaconda distribution, you could use `miniconda` (which we already covered earlier when discussing Numba's installation). With this approach, you can use the `conda` package manager by following these steps:

1. Create a new environment in which you can install a new version of Python using this line of code:

   ```
   $ conda create -n my_new_environment python
   ```

2. Enable that environment:

   ```
   $ source activate my_new_environment
   ```

3. Finally, install pandas:

   ```
   $ conda install  pandas
   ```

Additionally, pandas can be installed using the `pip` command-line tool (probably, the easiest and most compatible way of doing it) using this line of code:

```
$ pip install pandas
```

Finally, one more option could be installing it using your OS's package manager, given that the package is available:

Distribution	Repo link	Installation method
Debian	`packages.debian.org/search?keywords=pandas&searchon=names&suite=all&section=all`	`$ sudo apt-get install python-pandas`
Ubuntu	`http://packages.ubuntu.com/search?keywords=pandas&searchon=names&suite=all&section=all`	`$ sudo apt-get install python-pandas`
OpenSUSE and Fedora	`http://software.opensuse.org/package/python-pandas?search_term=pandas`	`$ zypper in python-pandas`

If the preceding options fail and you choose to install pandas from source, you can get the instructions from their website at `http://pandas.pydata.org/pandas-docs/stable/install.html`.

Using pandas for data analysis

In the world of big data and data analytics, having the right tools for the job means having the upper hand (of course, this is just one side of the story; the other one is knowing how to use them). For data analysis and, more specifically, for ad hoc tasks and data cleanup processes, one would normally use a programming language. A programming language would provide considerably more flexibility than a standard tool.

That being said, there are two languages that lead this particular performance race: R and Python. In the case of Python, this might come as a bit of a shock for some, since we've been showing nothing but evidence that Python by itself is not fast enough when it comes to number crunching. This is why libraries such as pandas are created.

It provides tools designed to ease and simplify the task commonly known as "data wrangling", such as:

- The ability to load big data files into memory and stream out
- Simple integration with `matplotlib` (`http://matplotlib.org/`), which enables it to create interactive plots with very few lines of code
- Simple syntax to deal with missing data, dropping fields, and so on

Let's now look at a very simple and quick example of how using pandas can benefit the performance of your code as well as improve the syntax of your programs. The following code grabs a CSV file, with a portion of the export (a 500 MB file) from **the 311 service requests from 2010 to present** taken from the NYC OpenData site (`https://data.cityofnewyork.us/Social-Services/311-Service-Requests-from-2010-to-Present/erm2-nwe9`).

It then tries to simply calculate the number of records per zip code using both plain Python and pandas code:

```
import pandas as pd
import time
import csv
import collections

SOURCE_FILE = './311.csv'

def readCSV(fname):
  with open(fname, 'rb') as csvfile:
    reader = csv.DictReader(csvfile)
    lines = [line for line in reader]
    return lines

def process(fname):
  content = readCSV(fname)
  incidents_by_zipcode = collections.defaultdict(int)
  for record in content:
    incidents_by_zipcode[toFloat(record['Incident Zip'])] += 1
  return sorted(incidents_by_zipcode.items(), reverse=True,
  key=lambda a: int(a[1]))[:10]

def toFloat(number):
  try:
    return int(float(number))
  except:
    return 0

def process_pandas(fname):
  df = pd.read_csv(fname, dtype={'Incident Zip': str, 'Landmark':
  str, 'Vehicle Type': str, 'Ferry Direction': str})

  df['Incident Zip'] = df['Incident Zip'].apply(toFloat)
  column_names =  list(df.columns.values)
  column_names.remove("Incident Zip")
```

```
    column_names.remove("Unique Key")
    return df.drop(column_names, axis=1).groupby(['Incident Zip'],
    sort=False).count().sort('Unique Key', ascending=False).head(10)

init = time.clock()
total = process(SOURCE_FILE)
endtime = time.clock() - init
for item in total:
  print "%s\t%s" % (item[0], item[1])

print "(Pure Python) time: %s" % (endtime)

init = time.clock()
total = process_pandas(SOURCE_FILE)
endtime = time.clock() - init
print total
print "(Pandas) time: %s" % (endtime)
```

The process function is very simple. It has only five lines of code. It loads the file, does a bit of processing (mainly manual grouping and counting), and finally, it sorts the results and returns the first 10 of them. As an added bonus, we use the defaultdict data type, which we mentioned a few chapters ago as a possible performance improvement in these cases.

On the other side, the process_pandas function does essentially the same thing, only with pandas. We have some more lines of code, but they are quite simple to understand. They're clearly "data-wrangling oriented", as you can see that there are no loops declared. We can even access the columns by name automatically and apply functions over those groups of records without having to manually iterate over them.

The following screenshot shows the output of the preceding code:

As you can see, there is a 3-second improvement on the performance of our algorithm when we simply reimplement it in pandas. Let's now dig a bit deeper into the API of pandas in order to get even better numbers. There are two major improvements we can make to our code, and they're both related to the `read_csv` method, which uses a lot of parameters. Two of these parameters are of real interest to us:

- `usecols`: This will only return the columns we want, effectively helping us deal with only 2 columns out of the 40+ our dataset has. This will also help us get rid of the logic that we have to drop the columns before returning the results.

- `converters`: This allows us to auto-convert data with a function, instead of calling the apply method, as we will do now.

Our new function looks like this:

```
def process_pandas(fname):
    df = pd.read_csv(fname, usecols=['Incident Zip', 'Unique Key'],
    converters={'Incident Zip': toFloat}, dtype={'Incident Zip':
    str})
    return df.groupby(['Incident Zip'],
    sort=False).count().sort('Unique Key', ascending=False).head(10)
```

That's right. Only two lines of code! The reader will do all the work for us. Then, we need to simply group, count, and sort. Now, check out how this looks compared to our previous results:

That's a 10-second improvement on the performance of our algorithm and considerably less code to deal with, otherwise known as a "win-win" situation.

An added bonus to our code is that it scales. The pandas-based function can deal with a 5.9 GB file in just 30 seconds with no changes. On the other hand, our pure Python code won't even load that file in that time, let alone process it if we don't have enough resources.

Parakeet

This one is the most specific tool yet to deal with numbers in Python. It is very specific because it only supports a very narrow subset of the resulting combination of Python and NumPy. So, if you're dealing with anything outside that universe, this might not be an option for you, but if you can fit your solution into it, then keep on reading.

To be more specific about the limited universe that Parakeet supports (normally useful only to express numerical computations), here is a short list:

- Types supported by Python are numbers, tuples, slices, and NumPy's arrays
- Parakeet follows the upcasting rule, that is, whenever two values of different types try to reach the same variable, they'll be upcast into a unifying one. For instance, the Python expression `1.0 if b else false` would translate to `1.0 if b else 0.0`, but when automatic casting isn't possible, such as `1.0 if b else (1,2)`, then an uncatchable exception (see next point) will be raised during compilation time.
- Catching or even raising exceptions isn't possible in Parakeet; neither are break and continue statements. This is because Parakeet represents programs using structured SSA (`http://citeseerx.ist.psu.edu/viewdoc/summary?doi=10.1.1.45.4503`).
- Array broadcasting (a feature of NumPy) is partially implemented by inserting explicit map operators based on the types of array arguments. This is a limited implementation because it can't really handle an expansion of dimensions (such as broadcasting 8 x 2 x 3 and 7 x 2 arrays).
- There is only a small subset of the built-in functions of Python and NumPy that have been implemented. The complete list can be seen at `https://github.com/iskandr/parakeet/blob/master/parakeet/mappings.py`.
- List comprehension expressions are treated as array comprehensions.

Installing Parakeet

The installation of Parakeet is simple enough. There are no hard-to-get requirements if you want to go with the `pip` route. Simply type the following command:

```
$ pip install parakeet
```

And you're done!

If, on the other hand, you want to directly try the source code approach, you would need some other packages installed beforehand. Here is a list of these packages:

- **Python 2.7**
- **dsltools** (`https://github.com/iskandr/dsltools`)
- **nose** for running the tests (`https://nose.readthedocs.org/en/latest/`)
- **NumPy** (`http://www.scipy.org/install.html`)
- **appDirs** (`https://pypi.python.org/pypi/appdirs/`)
- **gcc 4.4+** for the OpenMP back-end, which is the default one

If you're on a Windows box, you would have better luck if it's a 32-bit machine. Otherwise, you might be out of luck since there is no official documentation on the subject.

If you are a OS X user you'll probably want to install a more up-to-date version of the C compiler using HomeBrew, since either clang or the installed version of `gcc` might not be updated enough.

After the prerequisites are met, simply download the code from: `https://github.com/iskandr/parakeet` and run the following command (from within the code's folder):

```
$ python setup.py install
```

How does Parakeet work?

Instead of going deep into the details about the theory behind Parakeet, let's simply see how to use it to optimize our code. This will help you get a feel of the module without having to chew through all the documentation.

The main construct of this library is a decorator that you can apply to your functions, so Parakeet can take control and optimize your code if possible.

For our simple test, let's take one of the example functions presented on Parakeet's website and run a simple test against a `4000 * 4000` random floating-point list. The code will run the same function in both an optimized way using Parakeet, and in an unoptimized way. Then, it will measure the time each one takes to process the exact same input:

```python
from parakeet import jit
import random
import numpy as np
import time

@jit
def allpairs_dist_prkt(X,Y):
  def dist(x,y):
    return np.sum( (x-y)**2 )
  return np.array([[dist(x,y) for y in Y] for x in X])

def allpairs_dist_py(X,Y):
  def dist(x,y):
    return np.sum( (x-y)**2 )
```

```
    return np.array([[dist(x,y) for y in Y] for x in X])

input_a = [ random.random() for x in range(0, 4000)]
input_b = [ random.random() for x in range(0, 4000)]

print "------------------------------------------------"
init = time.clock()
allpairs_dist_py(input_a, input_b)
end = time.clock()
print "Total time pure python: %s" % (end - init)
print
init = time.clock()
allpairs_dist_prkt(input_a, input_b)
end = time.clock()
print "Total time parakeet: %s" % (end - init)
print "------------------------------------------------"
```

In an i7 processor, with 8 GB of RAM, this is the performance we get:

```
------------------------------------------------
Total time pure python: 73.19119

Total time parakeet: 0.088978
------------------------------------------------
```

The preceding screenshot shows the amazing performance boost we get in this particular function (which complies with the required subset of Python supported by Parakeet).

Simply put, the decorated function is being used as a template from which several type-specialized functions are created, one for each input type (in our case, we only need one). It is these new functions that get optimized in several different ways by Parakeet before getting translated into native code.

 Note that even though the performance gain is amazing, Parakeet only supports a very limited version of Python, so it is not really meant to be a general purpose optimizer (quite the opposite actually).

Summary

In this chapter, we covered three alternatives to data processing with Python. We covered specific use cases (but with amazing benefits), such as Parakeet, and others more generic ones, such as pandas and Numba. For all three of them, we covered the basics: description, installation, and an example. There is a lot more to discover for each one, depending on your specific needs. However, the information provided here should be enough to start you in the right direction.

For the next and final chapter, we'll cover a practical example of a script in need of optimization. We'll try to apply everything (or as much as makes sense) that we've covered so far in the book.

8
Putting It All into Practice

Welcome to the last chapter of the book. If you've made it this far, you've gone over several optimization techniques, both specific to the Python programming language and generic ones applicable to other similar technologies.

You've also read about tools for profiling and visualizing those results. We also delved into one specific use case for Python, which is number crunching for scientific purposes. You learned about the tools that allow you to optimize the performance of your code.

In this final chapter, we'll go over one practical use case that covers all the technologies we covered in the earlier chapters (remember that some of the tools we've seen are alternatives, so using all of them is not really a good plan). We will write an initial version of the code, measure its performance, and then go through the optimization process to finally rewrite the code and measure the performance again.

The problem to solve

Before we even start thinking about writing the initial version of our code, we need to understand the problem we're trying to solve.

Given the scope of the book, a full-blown application might be too big an undertaking, so we'll focus on a small task. It'll give us better control over what we want to do, and we won't run the risk of having too many things to optimize at the same time.

To keep things interesting, we'll split the problem into the following two parts:

- **Part 1**: This will take care of finding the data we want to process. It won't just be a dataset we download from some given URL. Instead, we'll scrape it from the Web.

- **Part 2**: This will focus on processing the data obtained after solving the first part of the problem. In this step, we may perform the most CPU-intensive computations and calculate some statistics from the data gathered.

In both cases, we'll create an initial version of the code that solves the problem without taking performance into account. Afterwards, we'll analyze each solution individually and try to improve them as much as we can.

Getting data from the Web

The site we'll scrape is **Science Fiction & Fantasy** (`http://scifi.stackexchange.com/`). The site is dedicated to answering questions about sci-fi and fantasy topics. It is much like StackOverflow but meant for sci-fi and fantasy geeks.

To be more specific, we'll want to scrape the list of latest questions. For each question, we'll get the page with the question's text and all the available answers. After all the scraping and parsing is done, we'll save the relevant information in the JSON format for easier postprocessing.

Remember that we'll deal with HTML pages. However, we don't want that. We want to strip away all HTML code and save only the following items:

- The question's title
- The question's author
- The question's body (the actual text of the question)
- The body of the answers (if there are any)
- The answer's author

With this information, we'll be able to do some interesting postprocessing and get some relevant statistics (more on that in a minute).

Here is a quick example of how the output of this script should look:

```
{
    "questions": [
        {
            "title": "Ending of John Carpenter's The Thing",
            "body": "In the ending of John Carpenter's classic 1982 sci-
            fi horror film The Thing, is ...",
            "author": "JMFB",
            "answers": [
                {
                    "body": "This is the million dollar question, ...
                    Unfortunately, he is notoriously ... ",
                     "author": "Richard",
                },
                {

                    "body": "Not to point out what may seem obvious,
                    but Childs isn't breathing. Note the total absence of ",
                    "author": "user42"
                    }
            ]
        },
        {

            "title": "Was it ever revealed what pedaling the bicycles in
            the second episode was doing?",
            "body": "I'm going to assume they were probably some sort of
            turbine...electricity...something, but I'd prefer to know
            for sure.",
             "author": "bartz",
            "answers": [
                {
                    "body": "The Wikipedia synopsis states: most citizens
                    make a living pedaling exercise bikes all day in order
                    to generate power for their environment",
                    "author": "Jack Nimble"
                }
            ]
        }
    ]
}
```

This script will take care of saving all the information into one single JSON file, which will be predefined inside its code.

We'll try to keep the initial version of both scripts simple. This means using the least amount of modules. In this case, the main list of modules will be as follows:

- **Beautiful Soup** (`http://www.crummy.com/software/BeautifulSoup/`): This is used to parse the HTML files, mainly because it provides a full parsing API, automatic encoding detection (which, if you've being in this business long enough, you've probably come to hate) and the ability to use selectors to traverse the parsed tree.

- **Requests** (`http://docs.python-requests.org/en/latest/`): This is used to make HTTP requests. Although Python already provides the required modules for this, this module simplifies the API and provides a more Pythonic way of handling this task.

You can install both modules using the `pip` command-line tool:

```
$ pip  install requests  beautifulsoup4
```

The following screenshot shows an example of the pages we'll be scraping and parsing in order to get the data:

Postprocessing the data

The second script will take care of reading the JSON-encoded file and getting some stats out of it. Since we want to make it interesting, we won't limit ourselves to just counting the number of questions per user (although we will get this stat as well). We'll also calculate the following elements:

- Top ten users with most questions
- Top ten users with most answers
- Most common topics asked about
- The shortest answer
- Top ten most common phrases
- Top ten most answered questions

Since this book's main topic is performance and not **Natural Language Processing (NLP)**, we will not delve into the details of the small amount of NLP that this script will have. Instead, we'll just limit ourselves to improving the performance based on what we've seen so far about Python.

The only non-built-in module we'll use in the first version of this script is **NLTK** (http://www.nltk.org) to handle all the NLP functionalities.

The initial code base

Let's now list all of the code that we'll optimize in future, based on the earlier description.

The first of the following points is quite simple: a single file script that takes care of scraping and saving in JSON format like we discussed earlier. The flow is simple, and the order is as follows:

1. It will query the list of questions page by page.
2. For each page, it will gather the question's links.
3. Then, for each link, it will gather the information listed from the previous points.
4. It will move on to the next page and start over again.
5. It will finally save all of the data into a JSON file.

The code is as follows:

```
from bs4 import BeautifulSoup
import requests
import json


SO_URL = "http://scifi.stackexchange.com"
QUESTION_LIST_URL = SO_URL + "/questions"
MAX_PAGE_COUNT = 20

global_results = []
initial_page = 1 #first page is page 1

def get_author_name(body):
  link_name = body.select(".user-details a")
  if len(link_name) == 0:
    text_name = body.select(".user-details")
    return text_name[0].text if len(text_name) > 0 else 'N/A'
  else:
    return link_name[0].text

def get_question_answers(body):
  answers = body.select(".answer")
  a_data = []
  if len(answers) == 0:
    return a_data

  for a in answers:
    data = {
      'body': a.select(".post-text")[0].get_text(),
      'author': get_author_name(a)
    }
    a_data.append(data)
  return a_data

def get_question_data ( url ):
  print "Getting data from question page: %s " % (url)
  resp = requests.get(url)
  if resp.status_code != 200:
    print "Error while trying to scrape url: %s" % (url)
    return
  body_soup = BeautifulSoup(resp.text)
  #define the output dict that will be turned into a JSON structue
```

```python
    q_data = {
      'title': body_soup.select('#question-header .question-
      hyperlink')[0].text,
      'body': body_soup.select('#question .post-
      text')[0].get_text(),
      'author': get_author_name(body_soup.select(".post-
      signature.owner")[0]),
      'answers': get_question_answers(body_soup)
    }
    return q_data


def get_questions_page ( page_num, partial_results ):
  print "===================================================="
  print " Getting list of questions for page %s" % (page_num)
  print "===================================================="

  url = QUESTION_LIST_URL + "?sort=newest&page=" + str(page_num)
  resp = requests.get(url)
  if resp.status_code != 200:
    print "Error while trying to scrape url: %s" % (url)
    return
  body = resp.text
  main_soup = BeautifulSoup(body)

  #get the urls for each question
  questions = main_soup.select('.question-summary .question-
  hyperlink')
  urls = [ SO_URL + x['href'] for x in questions]
  for url in urls:
    q_data = get_question_data(url)
    partial_results.append(q_data)
  if page_num < MAX_PAGE_COUNT:
    get_questions_page(page_num + 1, partial_results)


get_questions_page(initial_page, global_results)
with open('scrapping-results.json', 'w') as outfile:
  json.dump(global_results, outfile, indent=4)

print '----------------------------------------------------'
print 'Results saved'
```

By looking at the preceding code, you'll notice that we kept our promise. Right now, we're only using the proposed external modules, plus the JSON module, which comes built-in with Python.

The second script, on the other hand, is split into two, mainly for organizational purposes:

- `analyzer.py`: This file contains the main code. It takes care of loading the JSON file into a `dict` structure and performs a series of calculations.
- `visualizer.py`: This file simply contains a set of functions used to visualize the different results from the analyzer.

Let's now take a look at the code in both these files. The first set of functions will be the utility functions used to sanitize the data, load it into memory, and so on:

```python
#analyzer.py
import operator
import string
import nltk
from nltk.util import ngrams
import json
import re
import visualizer


SOURCE_FILE = './scrapping-results.json'


# Load the json file and return the resulting dict
def load_json_data(file):
  with open(file) as input_file:
    return json.load(input_file)

def analyze_data(d):
  return {
    'shortest_answer': get_shortest_answer(d),
    'most_active_users': get_most_active_users(d, 10),
    'most_active_topics': get_most_active_topics(d, 10),
    'most_helpful_user': get_most_helpful_user(d, 10),
    'most_answered_questions': get_most_answered_questions(d, 10),
    'most_common_phrases':  get_most_common_phrases(d, 10, 4),
  }


# Creates a single, lower cased string from the bodies of all
questions
```

```
def flatten_questions_body(data):
  body = []
  for q in data:
    body.append(q['body'])
  return '. '.join(body)


# Creates a single, lower cased string from the titles of all
questions
def flatten_questions_titles(data):
  body = []
  pattern = re.compile('(\[|\])')
  for q in data:
    lowered = string.lower(q['title'])
    filtered = re.sub(pattern, ' ', lowered)
    body.append(filtered)
  return '. '.join(body)
```

The following set of functions are the ones that actually performs the *counting* of data and gets the statistics we want by analyzing the JSON in different ways:

```
# Returns the top "limit" users with the most questions asked
def get_most_active_users(data, limit):
  names = {}
  for q in data:
    if q['author'] not in names:
      names[q['author']] = 1
    else:
      names[q['author']] += 1
  return sorted(names.items(), reverse=True,
  key=operator.itemgetter(1))[:limit]


def get_node_content(node):
  return ' '.join([x[0] for x in node])


# Tries to extract the most common topics from the question's titles
def get_most_active_topics(data, limit):
  body = flatten_questions_titles(data)
  sentences = nltk.sent_tokenize(body)
  sentences = [nltk.word_tokenize(sent) for sent in sentences]
  sentences = [nltk.pos_tag(sent) for sent in sentences]
  grammar = "NP: {<JJ>?<NN.*>}"
  cp = nltk.RegexpParser(grammar)
  results = {}
  for sent in sentences:
```

```
      parsed = cp.parse(sent)
      trees = parsed.subtrees(filter=lambda x: x.label() == 'NP')
      for t in trees:
        key = get_node_content(t)
        if key in results:
          results[key] += 1
        else:
          results[key] = 1
    return sorted(results.items(), reverse=True, key=operator.
itemgetter(1))[:limit]


# Returns the user that has the most answers
def get_most_helpful_user(data, limit):
  helpful_users = {}
  for q in data:
    for a in q['answers']:
      if a['author'] not in helpful_users:
        helpful_users[a['author']] = 1
      else:
        helpful_users[a['author']] += 1

  return sorted(helpful_users.items(), reverse=True, key=operator.
itemgetter(1))[:limit]


# returns the top "limit" questions with the most amount of answers
def get_most_answered_questions(d, limit):
  questions = {}

  for q in d:
    questions[q['title']] = len(q['answers'])
  return sorted(questions.items(), reverse=True, key=operator.
itemgetter(1))[:limit]




# Finds a list of the most common phrases of 'length' length
def get_most_common_phrases(d, limit, length):
  body = flatten_questions_body(d)
  phrases = {}
  for sentence in nltk.sent_tokenize(body):
    words = nltk.word_tokenize(sentence)
    for phrase in ngrams(words, length):
      if all(word not in string.punctuation for word in phrase):
        key = ' '.join(phrase)
```

```
        if key in phrases:
           phrases[key] += 1
        else:
         phrases[key] = 1

  return sorted(phrases.items(), reverse=True,
  key=operator.itemgetter(1))[:limit]

# Finds the answer with the least amount of characters
def get_shortest_answer(d):

  shortest_answer = {
    'body': '',
    'length': -1
  }
  for q in d:
    for a in q['answers']:
      if len(a['body']) < shortest_answer['length'] or
      shortest_answer['length'] == -1:
        shortest_answer = {
           'question': q['body'],
           'body': a['body'],
           'length': len(a['body'])
        }
  return shortest_answer
```

The following code shows how to use the functions declared earlier and display their results. It all boils down to three steps:

1. It loads the JSON into memory.
2. It processes the data and saves the results into a dictionary.
3. It goes over that dictionary to display the results.

The preceding steps are performed in the following code:

```
data_dict = load_json_data(SOURCE_FILE)

results = analyze_data(data_dict)

print "=== ( Shortest Answer ) === "
visualizer.displayShortestAnswer(results['shortest_answer'])

print "=== ( Most Active Users ) === "
```

```
visualizer.displayMostActiveUsers(results['most_active_users'])

print "=== ( Most Active Topics ) === "
visualizer.displayMostActiveTopics(results['most_active_topics'])

print "=== ( Most Helpful Users ) === "
visualizer.displayMostHelpfulUser(results['most_helpful_user'])

print "=== ( Most Answered Questions ) === "
visualizer.displayMostAnsweredQuestions(results['most_answered_
questions'])

print "=== ( Most Common Phrases ) === "
visualizer.displayMostCommonPhrases(results['most_common_phrases'])
```

The code in the following file is merely used to format the output in a human-friendly way:

```
#visualizer.py
def displayShortestAnswer(data):
  print "A: %s" % (data['body'])
  print "Q: %s" % (data['question'])
  print "Length: %s characters" % (data['length'])

def displayMostActiveUsers(data):
  index = 1
  for u in data:
    print "%s - %s (%s)" % (index, u[0], u[1])
    index += 1

def displayMostActiveTopics(data):
  index = 1
  for u in data:
    print "%s - %s (%s)" % (index, u[0], u[1])
    index += 1

def displayMostHelpfulUser(data):
  index = 1
  for u in data:
    print "%s - %s (%s)" % (index, u[0], u[1])
    index += 1

def displayMostAnsweredQuestions(data):
  index = 1
  for u in data:
```

```
            print "%s - %s (%s)" % (index, u[0], u[1])
            index += 1

    def displayMostCommonPhrases(data):
        index = 1
        for u in data:
            print "%s - %s (%s)" % (index, u[0], u[1])
            index += 1
```

Analyzing the code

Analyzing the code will be done in two steps, just like we've being doing so far. For each project, we'll profile the code, get the numbers, consider our optimization alternatives, and then refactor and measure the code's performance again.

 As the process described earlier can lead to several iterations of profiling—refactoring—profiling again, we'll limit the steps to the final results. However, keep in mind that this process is long and takes time.

Scraper

To start off the optimization process, let's first get some measurements so that we can compare our changes with them.

An easy-to-get number is the total time spent during the program's execution (in our example, and to keep things simple, we're limiting the total number of pages to query to 20).

Simply using the `time` command-line tool, we can get that number:

```
$ time python scraper.py
```

The following screenshot shows that we have 7 minutes and 30 seconds to scrape and parse the 20 pages of questions, which translate into a 3 MB JSON file:

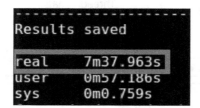

The scraper script is essentially an IO-bound loop that pulls data from the Internet with a minimum amount of processing. So, the first and most logical optimization we can spot here is the lack of parallelization of the requests. Since our code is not really CPU-bound, we can safely use the multithreading module (refer to *Chapter 5, Multithreading versus Multiprocessing*) and get an interesting speed boost with minimum effort.

Just to clarify what we're going to be doing, the following diagram shows the current status of the scraper script:

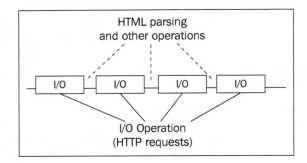

We're spending most of our running time on I/O operations, more specifically on the HTTP requests we're doing to get the list of questions and each question's page.

As we've seen earlier, I/O operations can be parallelized easily using the multithreading module. So, we will transform our script so it resembles as shown in the following diagram:

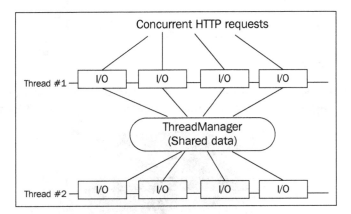

Now, let's look at the actual optimized code. We'll first look at the `ThreadManager` class, which will take care of centralizing the configuration of the threads as well as the status of the entire parallel process:

```
from bs4 import BeautifulSoup
import requests
import json
import threading


SO_URL = "http://scifi.stackexchange.com"
QUESTION_LIST_URL = SO_URL + "/questions"
MAX_PAGE_COUNT = 20


class ThreadManager:
  instance = None
  final_results = []
  threads_done = 0
  totalConnections = 4 #Number of parallel threads working, will
  affect the total amount of pages per thread

  @staticmethod
  def notify_connection_end( partial_results ):
    print "==== Thread is done! ====="
    ThreadManager.threads_done += 1
    ThreadManager.final_results += partial_results
    if ThreadManager.threads_done ==
    ThreadManager.totalConnections:
      print "==== Saving data to file! ===="
      with open('scrapping-results-optimized.json', 'w') as
      outfile:
        json.dump(ThreadManager.final_results, outfile, indent=4)
```

The following functions take care of scraping the information from a page using `BeatifulSoup`, either by getting the lists of pages or getting the actual information for each question:

```
def get_author_name(body):
  link_name = body.select(".user-details a")
  if len(link_name) == 0:
    text_name = body.select(".user-details")
    return text_name[0].text if len(text_name) > 0 else 'N/A'
  else:
```

```python
      return link_name[0].text

def get_question_answers(body):
  answers = body.select(".answer")
  a_data = []
  if len(answers) == 0:
    return a_data

  for a in answers:
    data = {
      'body': a.select(".post-text")[0].get_text(),
      'author': get_author_name(a)
    }
    a_data.append(data)
  return a_data


def get_question_data ( url ):
  print "Getting data from question page: %s " % (url)
  resp = requests.get(url)
  if resp.status_code != 200:
    print "Error while trying to scrape url: %s" % (url)
    return
  body_soup = BeautifulSoup(resp.text)
  #define the output dict that will be turned into a JSON structue
  q_data = {
    'title': body_soup.select('#question-header .question-
    hyperlink')[0].text,
    'body': body_soup.select('#question .post-
    text')[0].get_text(),
    'author': get_author_name(body_soup.select(".post-
    signature.owner")[0]),
    'answers': get_question_answers(body_soup)
  }
  return q_data


def get_questions_page ( page_num, end_page, partial_results ):
  print "===================================================="
  print " Getting list of questions for page %s" % (page_num)
  print "===================================================="

  url = QUESTION_LIST_URL + "?sort=newest&page=" + str(page_num)
  resp = requests.get(url)
```

```
if resp.status_code != 200:
  print "Error while trying to scrape url: %s" % (url)
else:
  body = resp.text
  main_soup = BeautifulSoup(body)

  #get the urls for each question
  questions = main_soup.select('.question-summary .question-
  hyperlink')
  urls = [ SO_URL + x['href'] for x in questions]
  for url in urls:
    q_data = get_question_data(url)
    partial_results.append(q_data)
  if page_num + 1 < end_page:
    get_questions_page(page_num + 1, end_page, partial_results)
  else:
    ThreadManager.notify_connection_end(partial_results)
pages_per_connection = MAX_PAGE_COUNT / ThreadManager.totalConnections
for i in range(ThreadManager.totalConnections):
  init_page = i * pages_per_connection
  end_page = init_page + pages_per_connection
  t = threading.Thread(target=get_questions_page,
          args=(init_page, end_page, [], ),
          name='connection-%s' % (i))
  t.start()
```

The highlighted code in the preceding snippet shows the main change done to the initial script. Instead of starting at page 1 and moving forward one by one, we're starting a preconfigured number of threads (using the threading.Thread class directly) that will call our get_question_page function in parallel. All we had to do was pass in that function as the target of each new thread.

After that, we also needed a way to centralize the configuration parameters and the temporary results from each thread. For that, we created the ThreadManager class.

With this change, we go from the 7 minutes mark all the way down to 2 minutes 13 seconds, as shown in the following screenshot:

```
real    2m13.450s
user    1m9.068s
sys     0m5.031s
```

Tweaking the number of threads, for instance, might lead to even better numbers, but the main improvement is already there.

Analyzer

The code for the analyzer script is different compared to the scraper. Instead of having a heavy I/O-bound script, we have the opposite: a CPU-bound one. It does very little I/O, mainly to read the input file and output the results. So, we will focus on measuring in more detail.

Let's first get some basic measurements so that we know where we stand:

The preceding screenshot shows the output of the time command-line utility. So now that we have a base number to work with, we know we need to get the execution time lower than 3.5 seconds.

The first approach would be to use cProfile and start getting some numbers from the inside of our code. This should help us get a general overview of our program to start understanding where our pain points are. The output looks like the following screenshot:

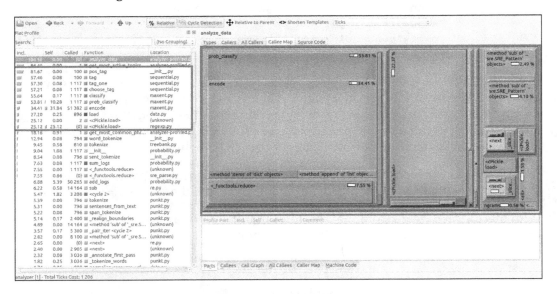

There are two areas of interest in the preceding screenshot:

- On the left-hand side, we can see the functions and how much time they consume. Pay attention to how most of the list is composed of external functions, mainly from the `nltk` module (the first two are just consumers of the others below, so they don't really matter).

- On the right-hand side, the **Callee Map** looks way too complex to interpret it (quite apart from the fact that again, most of the functions listed there aren't from our code, but from the libraries we're using).

With that being said, it looks like improving our code directly is not going to be a simple task. Instead, we might want to go on another route: since we're doing a lot of counting, we might benefit from typed code. So, let's try our hand at using Cython.

An initial analysis using the Cython command-line utility shows that most of our code can't directly be translated into C, as shown in the following screenshot:

```
Generated by Cython 0.22

Raw output: analyzer.c

+001: import operator
+002: import string
+003: import nltk
+004: from nltk.util import ngrams
+005: import json
+006: import re
+007: import visualizer
 008:
 009:
+010: SOURCE_FILE = './scrapping-results.json'
 011:
 012: # Returns the top "limit" users with the most questions asked
+013: def get_most_active_users(data, limit):
+014:     names = {}
+015:     for q in data:
+016:         if q['author'] not in names:
+017:             names[q['author']] = 1
 018:         else:
+019:             names[q['author']] += 1
+020:     return sorted(names.items(), reverse=True, key=operator.itemgetter(1))[:limit]
 021:
+022: def get_node_content(node):
+023:     return ' '.join([x[0] for x in node])
 024:
 025: # Tries to extract the most common topics from the question's titles
+026: def get_most_active_topics(data, limit):
+027:     body = flatten_questions_titles(data)
+028:     sentences = nltk.sent_tokenize(body)
+029:     sentences = [nltk.word_tokenize(sent) for sent in sentences]
+030:     sentences = [nltk.pos_tag(sent) for sent in sentences]
+031:     grammar = "NP: {<JJ>?<NN.*>}"
+032:     cp = nltk.RegexpParser(grammar)
+033:     results = {}
+034:     for sent in sentences:
+035:         parsed = cp.parse(sent)
+036:         trees = parsed.subtrees(filter=lambda x: x.label() == 'NP')
+037:         for t in trees:
+038:             key = get_node_content(t)
+039:             if key in results:
+040:                 results[key] += 1
 041:             else:
+042:                 results[key] = 1
+043:     return sorted(results.items(), reverse=True, key=operator.itemgetter(1))[:limit]
 044:
 045: # Returns the user that has the most answers
+046: def get_most_helpful_user(data, limit):
```

The preceding screenshot shows a portion of the analysis of our code. We can clearly see the darker lines filling most of the screen, showing that most of our code can't be directly translated into C. Sadly, this is because we're dealing with a complex object in most of our functions, so there isn't much we can do about it.

Still, simply by compiling our code with Cython, we get much better results. So, let's take a look at how we need to modify the source so that we can compile it with Cython. The first file is basically the same as the original analyzer with the changes highlighted in the code and minus the actual function calls, as we're now turning it into an external library:

```python
#analyzer_cython.pyx
import operator
import string
import nltk
from nltk.util import ngrams
import json
import re


SOURCE_FILE = './scrapping-results.json'

# Returns the top "limit" users with the most questions asked
def get_most_active_users(data, int limit ):
  names = {}
  for q in data:
    if q['author'] not in names:
      names[q['author']] = 1
    else:
      names[q['author']] += 1
  return sorted(names.items(), reverse=True, key=operator.
itemgetter(1))[:limit]

def get_node_content(node):
  return ' '.join([x[0] for x in node])

# Tries to extract the most common topics from the question's titles
def get_most_active_topics(data, int limit ):
  body = flatten_questions_titles(data)
  sentences = nltk.sent_tokenize(body)
  sentences = [nltk.word_tokenize(sent) for sent in sentences]
  sentences = [nltk.pos_tag(sent) for sent in sentences]
  grammar = "NP: {<JJ>?<NN.*>}"
  cp = nltk.RegexpParser(grammar)
```

```
    results = {}
    for sent in sentences:
      parsed = cp.parse(sent)
      trees = parsed.subtrees(filter=lambda x: x.label() == 'NP')
      for t in trees:
        key = get_node_content(t)
        if key in results:
          results[key] += 1
        else:
          results[key] = 1
    return sorted(results.items(), reverse=True,
    key=operator.itemgetter(1))[:limit]


# Returns the user that has the most answers
def get_most_helpful_user(data, int limit ):
  helpful_users = {}
  for q in data:
    for a in q['answers']:
      if a['author'] not in helpful_users:
        helpful_users[a['author']] = 1
      else:
        helpful_users[a['author']] -= 1

  return sorted(helpful_users.items(), reverse=True,
  key=operator.itemgetter(1))[:limit]


# returns the top "limit" questions with the most amount of answers
def get_most_answered_questions(d, int limit ):
  questions = {}

  for q in d:
    questions[q['title']] = len(q['answers'])
  return sorted(questions.items(), reverse=True,
  key=operator.itemgetter(1))[:limit]


# Creates a single, lower cased string from the bodies of all
questions
def flatten_questions_body(data):
  body = []
  for q in data:
    body.append(q['body'])
```

```python
    return '. '.join(body)


# Creates a single, lower cased string from the titles of all
questions
def flatten_questions_titles(data):
  body = []
  pattern = re.compile('(\[|\])')
  for q in data:
    lowered = string.lower(q['title'])
    filtered = re.sub(pattern, ' ', lowered)
    body.append(filtered)
  return '. '.join(body)

# Finds a list of the most common phrases of 'length' length
def get_most_common_phrases(d, int limit , int length ):
  body = flatten_questions_body(d)
  phrases = {}
  for sentence in nltk.sent_tokenize(body):
    words = nltk.word_tokenize(sentence)
    for phrase in ngrams(words, length):
      if all(word not in string.punctuation for word in phrase):
        key = ' '.join(phrase)
        if key in phrases:
          phrases[key] += 1
        else:
          phrases[key] = 1


  return sorted(phrases.items(), reverse=True,
  key=operator.itemgetter(1))[:limit]

# Finds the answer with the least amount of characters
def get_shortest_answer(d):
  cdef int shortest_length = 0;

  shortest_answer = {
    'body': '',
    'length': -1
  }
  for q in d:
    for a in q['answers']:
```

```
    if len(a['body']) < shortest_length or shortest_length == 0:
        shortest_length = len(a['body'])
    shortest_answer = {
        'question': q['body'],
        'body': a['body'],
        'length': shortest_length
    }
return shortest_answer

# Load the json file and return the resulting dict
def load_json_data(file):
    with open(file) as input_file:
        return json.load(input_file)


def analyze_data(d):
    return {
        'shortest_answer': get_shortest_answer(d),
        'most_active_users': get_most_active_users(d, 10),
        'most_active_topics': get_most_active_topics(d, 10),
        'most_helpful_user': get_most_helpful_user(d, 10),
        'most_answered_questions': get_most_answered_questions(d, 10),
        'most_common_phrases':  get_most_common_phrases(d, 10, 4),
    }
```

The following file is the one that takes care of setting everything up for Cython to compile our code, we've seen this code before (refer to *Chapter 6, Generic Optimization Options*):

```
#analyzer-setup.py
from distutils.core import setup
from Cython.Build import cythonize

setup(
  name = 'Analyzer app',
  ext_modules = cythonize("analyzer_cython.pyx"),
)
```

The last file is the one that uses our new external library by importing the compiled module. The file calls on the `load_json_data` and `analyze_data` methods and, finally, uses the visualizer module to format the output:

```
#analyzer-use-cython.py
import analyzer_cython as analyzer
import visualizer


data_dict = analyzer.load_json_data(analyzer.SOURCE_FILE)

results = analyzer.analyze_data(data_dict)

print "=== ( Shortest Answer ) === "
visualizer.displayShortestAnswer(results['shortest_answer'])

print "=== ( Most Active Users ) === "
visualizer.displayMostActiveUsers(results['most_active_users'])

print "=== ( Most Active Topics ) === "
visualizer.displayMostActiveTopics(results['most_active_topics'])

print "=== ( Most Helpful Users ) === "
visualizer.displayMostHelpfulUser(results['most_helpful_user'])

print "=== ( Most Answered Questions ) === "
visualizer.displayMostAnsweredQuestions(results['most_answered_
questions'])

print "=== ( Most Common Phrases ) === "
visualizer.displayMostCommonPhrases(results['most_common_phrases'])
```

The preceding code can be compiled using the following line:

```
$ python analyzer-setup.py build_ext -inplace
```

Then, by running the `analyzer-use-cython.py` script, we will get the following execution time:

The time went down from 3.5 to 1.3 seconds. This is quite an improvement from simply reorganizing of our code and compiling it using Cython, like we saw in *Chapter 6, Generic Optimization Options*. This simple compilation can produce great results.

The code can be further broken down and rewritten to remove most of the need for complex structures, thus allowing us to declare the primitive types for all variables. We could even try to remove `nltk` and use some NLP library written in C, such as OpenNLP (`http://opennlp.sourceforge.net/projects.html`).

Summary

You've reached the end of the chapter and, with it, the end of this book. The examples provided in this last chapter are meant to show how a random piece of code can be analyzed and improved using the techniques shown in the previous chapters.

As not all techniques are compatible with each other, not all of them were applicable here. However, we were able to see how some of them work, more specifically, multithreading, profiling with `cProfile` and `kcachegrind`, and finally, compilation with Cython.

Thank you for reading and, hopefully, enjoying the book!

Index

stdname sort
  versus nfl sort 36
string concatenation 119-123

T

threading module
  event construct, URL 141
  thread class, URL 136
  working with 136-141
threads
  about 130
  creating, thread module used 131-136
  in Python 130
  interthread communication,
      with events 142, 143
  threading module 130
  thread module 130
tracing profilers 3

W

wxPython
  URL 83

Thank you for buying
Mastering Python High Performance

About Packt Publishing

Packt, pronounced 'packed', published its first book, *Mastering phpMyAdmin for Effective MySQL Management*, in April 2004, and subsequently continued to specialize in publishing highly focused books on specific technologies and solutions.

Our books and publications share the experiences of your fellow IT professionals in adapting and customizing today's systems, applications, and frameworks. Our solution-based books give you the knowledge and power to customize the software and technologies you're using to get the job done. Packt books are more specific and less general than the IT books you have seen in the past. Our unique business model allows us to bring you more focused information, giving you more of what you need to know, and less of what you don't.

Packt is a modern yet unique publishing company that focuses on producing quality, cutting-edge books for communities of developers, administrators, and newbies alike. For more information, please visit our website at www.packtpub.com.

About Packt Open Source

In 2010, Packt launched two new brands, Packt Open Source and Packt Enterprise, in order to continue its focus on specialization. This book is part of the Packt Open Source brand, home to books published on software built around open source licenses, and offering information to anybody from advanced developers to budding web designers. The Open Source brand also runs Packt's Open Source Royalty Scheme, by which Packt gives a royalty to each open source project about whose software a book is sold.

Writing for Packt

We welcome all inquiries from people who are interested in authoring. Book proposals should be sent to author@packtpub.com. If your book idea is still at an early stage and you would like to discuss it first before writing a formal book proposal, then please contact us; one of our commissioning editors will get in touch with you.

We're not just looking for published authors; if you have strong technical skills but no writing experience, our experienced editors can help you develop a writing career, or simply get some additional reward for your expertise.

Python High Performance Programming

ISBN: 978-1-78328-845-8   Paperback: 108 pages

Boost the performance of your Python programs using advanced techniques

1. Identify the bottlenecks in your applications and solve them using the best profiling techniques.

2. Write efficient numerical code in NumPy and Cython.

3. Adapt your programs to run on multiple processors with parallel programming.

Expert Python Programming

ISBN: 978-1-84719-494-7   Paperback: 372 pages

Best practices for designing, coding, and distributing your Python software

1. Learn Python development best practices from an expert, with detailed coverage of naming and coding conventions.

2. Apply object-oriented principles, design patterns, and advanced syntax tricks.

3. Manage your code with distributed version control.

Please check **www.PacktPub.com** for information on our titles

Learning Python Data Visualization

ISBN: 978-1-78355-333-4   Paperback: 212 pages

Master how to build dynamic HTML5-ready SVG charts using Python and the pygal library

1. A practical guide that helps you break into the world of data visualization with Python.

2. Understand the fundamentals of building charts in Python.

3. Packed with easy-to-understand tutorials for developers who are new to Python or charting in Python.

Python Network Programming Cookbook

ISBN: 978-1-84951-346-3   Paperback: 234 pages

Over 70 detailed recipes to develop practical solutions for a wide range of real-world network programming tasks

1. Demonstrates how to write various besopke client/server networking applications using standard and popular third-party Python libraries.

2. Learn how to develop client programs for networking protocols such as HTTP/HTTPS, SMTP, POP3, FTP, CGI, XML-RPC, SOAP and REST.

Please check **www.PacktPub.com** for information on our titles